CHATHAM HOUSE PAPERS

From Glasnost to Freedom of Speech

Russian Openness and International Relations

David Wedgwood Benn

The Royal Institute of International Affairs

Pinter Publishers
London

© Royal Institute of International Affairs, 1992

First published in Great Britain in 1992 by
Pinter Publishers Limited
25 Floral Street, London WC2E 9DS

British Library Cataloguing in Publication Data

A CIP catalogue record for this book is available from the British Library

ISBN 0-85567 007 0 (Paperback)
      0-85567 006 2 (Hardback)

Reproduced from copy supplied by
Koinonia Limited
Printed and bound in Great Britain by
Biddles Ltd

CONTENTS

CHATHAM HOUSE PAPERS

A Russian and CIS Programme Publication
Programme Director: Neil Malcolm

The Royal Institute of International Affairs, at Chatham House in London, has provided an impartial forum for discussion and debate on current international issues for some 70 years. Its resident research fellows, specialized information resources, and range of publications, conferences, and meetings span the fields of international politics, economics, and security. The Institute is independent of government.

Chatham House Papers are short monographs on current policy problems which have been commissioned by the RIIA. In preparing the papers, authors are advised by a study group of experts convened by the RIIA, and publication of a paper indicates that the Institute regards it as an authoritative contribution to the public debate. The Institute does not, however, hold opinions of its own; the views expressed in this publication are the responsibility of the author. The paper is published under the auspices of the Soviet Programme, funded by the ESRC (grant no. E 00 22 2011).

PREFACE

Anyone writing about the former Soviet Union over recent months has faced unusual problems: a constant need to update the manuscript to keep up with fast-moving events and, at one point, an uncertainty even about the name of the country which one was writing about.

In these unusual circumstances, I had special reason to appreciate the help given me by members of the Royal Institute of International Affairs. My thanks are due, above all, to Neil Malcolm, the head of the Institute's Soviet Programme, who originally suggested the idea of this study and who guided the manuscript through its various drafts, whilst frequently drawing my attention to new material which I would otherwise have missed. Particular thanks are due to Pauline Wickham, the Head of Publications, for piloting the manuscript through its editorial stages and for suggesting stylistic improvements on the way. I am also indebted to Margaret May of the Publications Department for her help with the incorporation of amendments to the manuscript; to the staff of the Chatham House Library; and, not least, to Shyama Iyer, the Soviet Programme Assistant, for her help in circulating earlier drafts of this paper and in making arrangements for me to visit Moscow.

The ideas in this paper were greatly stimulated by two study groups held at the Institute in 1991. I would like to express appreciation to all who took part and in particular to Graham Beel, Steve Crawshaw, Chris Cviic, Stephen Dalziel, Iain Elliot, Michael Herman, Sir Curtis

Keeble, Martin Nicholson, Riita Pittman, Daphne Skillen, Geoffrey Stern and Jonathan Stern. Outside the Institute I was also helped on specific points by John Tusa (on the growth of satellite television), by David Ostry (on the Russian audience for the BBC) and by James Michael (on the international law governing communications). I gained helpful insights from participating in a series of seminars, at the Institute of Historical Research in London, on 'The Cold War as History', to which Peter Hennessy kindly invited me. Besides that, I had the advantage of being able to consult Russian and English press material at the BBC World Service in Bush House. I was especially grateful to Stephen White and Margot Light for their detailed written comments on the manuscript, as well as for the material which they both provided. The opinions expressed here are of course entirely my own.

While working on this paper I had the opportunity, in June 1991, to visit Moscow as the guest of the Institute of World Economy and International Relations. My thanks are due to Professor Sergei Peregudov, Professor Efim Khesin and Alexander Shedrin for their hospitality, for their help in arranging further contacts in Moscow and for the talks we had.

Last but not least I owe thanks to my wife June for her forbearance in recent months – and apologies for interrupting our summer holiday after the Moscow coup of August last year.

March 1992   David Wedgwood Benn

1
INTRODUCTION: THE SOVIET MEDIA PRE-1985

In the early 1960s, a former British ambassador to Moscow, Sir William Hayter, defined the agenda for East-West relations as being 'to search for ways of living safely in an inevitably divided world'.[1] In relation to the cold war era, this dictum seemed extremely apposite. But today it clearly no longer holds good. For whatever the uncertainties of the post- cold war world may be, the fact of irreversible change is no longer in doubt.

The origins of that change came from within the Soviet Union, where, between 1985 and 1991, the political mould was decisively broken, despite the sometimes acute turmoil. The change was itself connected, in a crucially important way, with what came to be known as 'glasnost', often translated as 'openness'. Today that term has been to all intents and purposes superseded, and in any case there has been disagreement as to what precisely it meant. The point which concerns us here is that – by degrees after 1985 – the Soviet media became freer, the flow of inform- ation between Russia* and the West increased enormously in both directions, and the chance arose for a vast proliferation of unofficial

*Although every effort has been made to achieve maximum precision in distinguishing between the words 'Russian' and 'Soviet' and between 'Russia' and 'the USSR', complete precision has been impossible owing to the present state of flux. The meaning should, however, be clear from the particular context in each case.

contacts between Westerners and Russians. It is in this sense that the term 'openness' is used throughout this volume. The reality of the new Soviet openness gradually became obvious to more and more people – not only to experts but to millions of television viewers in the outside world, who got the chance to see and judge this new phenomenon for themselves.

The impact of openness on Soviet society itself has been extensively discussed.[2] The purpose of what follows here is to look specifically at some of the likely *international* consequences of openness – the consequences not only of Russia's unprecedented exposure to ideas from the West, but also of the outside world's new access to information about the former Soviet Union. Domestic and international factors are, needless to say, very closely interdependent, not unlike a chain of reflecting mirrors. For example, it was clear already by the late 1980s that changes in the USSR were modifying earlier Western stereotypes of the Soviet Union. Changes in Western attitudes were, in turn, having some impact on Soviet domestic developments. On the other hand, the new openness – particularly because of its revelations about the Soviet past – was contributing to the turmoil in Soviet society itself; and this in turn contributed to Western doubts about the country's stability. Assuming that Russia, or the former USSR, remains an open society, it is reasonable to expect this two-way process of interaction to continue as well.

Before we embark on a discussion of these issues, one preliminary question needs to be tackled. This is the problem of disentangling the role of information and the media from among all the other factors which shape events. No one imagines that the revolution in Eastern Europe in 1989, the revolution in the USSR two years later and the ending of the cold war were brought about solely by freedom of information or by the media. All the same it is hard to deny that openness was an essential ingredient in what happened: that without greater openness, the changes could never have occurred so soon or in such a relatively non-violent way. For example, the ending of the traditional Soviet secrecy contributed powerfully to the ending of the cold war – because Soviet secrecy in the past had helped to sustain the Western belief in a Soviet threat.

Information and the media are certainly not all-powerful in themselves. The best proof of this was the ultimate failure of the Soviet propaganda apparatus. Nevertheless, information which caters for an audience need or demand can make a powerful impact. This helps to explain the influence of foreign broadcasts on closed societies. It also helps to explain the role of the media in the post-1985 Soviet reforms. Indeed, where recent events in the former USSR are concerned, there are strong grounds for claiming that the media, both domestic and foreign, were of key importance – not just as reporters but as participants. This was clearly highlighted during the failed coup of August 1991, when listening to foreign broadcasts in the Soviet Union rapidly increased.

The role of information is so fundamentally important in the shaping of political perceptions that one is sometimes in danger of overlooking it. In his classic book on *Public Opinion*, Walter Lippmann highlighted this point by describing an imaginary scenario of British and German settlers living on a remote island at the time of the outbreak of the First World War. They remained on friendly terms for some time after the war had begun – because they at first knew nothing about it, owing to the delay in the delivery of newspapers.[3] It has also been observed, in a different context, that 'all reform begins with new information'. The saying comes not from any Soviet politician, but from the American consumer rights campaigner Ralph Nader, and dates back to the 1960s or 1970s.[4] It would be difficult to imagine any more powerful illustration of this maxim than the experience of Soviet glasnost after 1985.

With regard to the role of the media in the USSR, a further point has to be remembered. Recent decades have seen a worldwide technological revolution in communications, which was proceeding apace quite irrespective of Soviet reforms or the lack of them. The interaction between the two is itself a matter of some importance. The mass media's role today is immeasurably more powerful than it was after the revolution of February 1917 broke out, which was the last time that genuine freedom of speech and of the press had existed in Russia. In 1917, radio (except in the form of morse-code signals) and television had not come into being; and there were no more than two copies of newspapers per hundred inhabitants in a society where illiteracy was still widespread.[5] In 1920, when Bertrand Russell visited the Russian countryside, he found that the peasants were for the most part unaware of the allied blockade against Bolshevik Russia which was then in force, and that they had never even heard of Great Britain.[6] Today radio and television in Russia and its former territories are all but universal; and the population is totally literate and better educated than at any time in the country's history. The domestic implications of this fact are enormous. So too are the implications at the international level – because members of the public in the outside world now have a better opportunity than at any time in history to get prompt and first-hand information as to what is happening in Russia. In short, Russia's openness, quite apart from anything else, could mean an enormous leap towards a new international information age.

It would probably be wrong to coin any one term to describe Russian society today, if only because of the uncertainty as to where that society is going. But one thing seems beyond dispute. Prior to 1985, the USSR was – in some respects – more of a closed society than Nazi Germany in the 1930s. Germans, up to the outbreak of the Second World War, were still able to make private trips abroad, to stay in private homes when abroad, and to subscribe to foreign newspapers.[7] Foreign visitors to Nazi Germany could also stay in private homes. None of these things were generally true of Soviet Russia prior to 1985. However, by 1991, already on the eve of the failed coup, all this had changed. The USSR had in most respects become a much more open society than either Franco's Spain or Tito's Yugoslavia, both of which were sometimes favourably compared with the Soviet Union in the past because of their 'non-totalitarian' systems of rule. One of the main surviving restrictions on the rights of Soviet citizens – that relating to foreign travel and emigration – had been removed in principle by a new Soviet law approved in May 1991. In the following month, genuinely contested presidential elections were held in Russia; and it had already become perfectly possible to use the media to demand the resignation of the then Head of State, Mikhail Gorbachev. Nothing like this would been conceivable under Franco or Tito. Such was the magnitude of the change brought about under the umbrella term 'glasnost'.

The international consequences of this Russian openness could themselves be far-reaching. Indeed, the vista which they seem to open up for international relations is so enormous that they might arguably merit a case-study – even if the Iron Curtain were to descend once again. However, any discussion of this subject necessarily has to begin with the past and with the Soviet domestic scene. How did the pre-1985 system of information control in the USSR operate? How did glasnost originate? What was it supposed to mean, how did it evolve – and can the new media freedom in the former USSR be expected to last?

4

Only after these questions have been dealt with can one begin to assess the significance of the new openness for international relations. The rest of this chapter is therefore devoted to a brief backward glance at way the Soviet media were run prior to 1985, and at the almost unbroken historical Russian tradition of secrecy. This provides a benchmark against which the extent of change can be measured.

Chapter 2 looks at the origins of glasnost after Gorbachev's accession to power in 1985. These are sometimes forgotten amidst the welter of fast-moving events. Nevertheless, they are still of importance – as a means of casting light on the thinking of the post-1985 Soviet leaders.

Chapter 3 looks at the changes in Soviet media policy after 1985, paying particular attention to the new media legislation passed in and after 1990, and the state of media freedom up to the spring of 1992.

Chapter 4 will then examine some of the entirely new opportunities for contact between citizens of the former USSR and foreigners which glasnost has made possible. It will also look at a distinct but nevertheless related question, namely the steady development of international broadcasting in recent decades, which has now brought the world across the threshold of international television broadcasting by satellite.

Chapter 5 discusses the danger that openness or media freedom could 'turn sour'. Although originally introduced by Gorbachev as a lever for radical change, glasnost to a considerable degree proved to be double-edged. The flood of fresh, and often negative, information had a destabilizing effect and contributed to a general crisis of authority. Coming as it did at a time of economic crisis, growing inter-ethnic tensions and widespread talk of social collapse, openness or media freedom, for all its immensely positive results, helped to produce a domestic turmoil without precedent since the Stalin era. Doubts about the survival of democracy have been expressed in some quarters, even after the demise of the USSR. All of this carries a serious risk of negative international repercussions. Chaos in the ex-Soviet Union could, needless to say, make it harder for the West to assist current reforms. At worst, the turmoil could result in a strong authoritarian backlash in Russia itself.

Finally, Chapters 6, 7 and 8 turn to the possible international implications of Russian openness. The influence of Western ideas on the (former) USSR has of course been enormous: it is no exaggeration to say that (thanks very largely to the media) Russia is at present more exposed to ideas from the outside world than at any time in its history. This itself is a topic which calls for exploration. But the question also arises as to what the consequences of Russian openness are likely to be for the West. From the foreign observer's point of view, the traditional dearth of information has now been replaced by an information glut. How is this affecting the way in which we interpret Russian affairs? What impact has it had, or might it have, on the political climate in the West? And, in conclusion, if this openness continues, how far will its international consequences be automatic, and how far will they require policy choices for the West and for Britain in particular?

The historical background

The Russian tradition of isolation, state secrecy and control over the press is notorious; and in certain important ways it predated the Bolshevik Revolution. Prior to the First World War, Russia was the only European country which required foreign visitors to have a passport. The Tsarist law on censorship, in force up to 1917, laid down a whole series of prohibitions on what might be published; and gave the authorities a discretionary power, during periods of emergency, to suspend newspapers altogether. To all this was added the wartime censorship after 1914, which gave rise to a significant number of clandestine newspapers.[8] One of the leading British experts on Tsarist Russia, Sir Bernard Pares, who had known the country since 1899, noted that even before the Revolution, Russia had been, to an abnormal extent, cut off from the outside world. This isolation, as Pares pointed out, was made all the greater by the unfamiliarity of most foreigners with the Russian language:

> Before the Revolution the British Embassy was practically interned. There was light social converse, but our representatives were not expected to inquire into the conditions of the country. The government of the Tsars kept a number of fashionable young attachés who talked perfect English with a public school accent, and gave facile and hopelessly misleading information. These were sent flying by the Revolution; and our own attachés, ignorant of Russian, complained that the new officials 'talked no known language' – only, that is, the language of their own country.[9]

The 'internment' of foreign embassies became much more complete after the Bolshevik Revolution, as Pares himself went on to point out, partly because Russians found it inadvisable to visit foreign embassies. Foreign correspondents in Russia became a rarity: *The Times* during the interwar years had no Moscow correspondent.[10] W. H. Chamberlin, who reported from the USSR for the *Christian Science Monitor* from 1922 to 1934, later recalled that foreign journalists in Moscow at that time 'could learn ... only a small part of the truth and ... could communicate ... only a fraction of what they knew'.[11] Paradoxically, or so it might seem, the information barrier was in some ways greater under Khrushchev in the 1950s than under Stalin up to the mid-1930s. The reason for this was that, during the earlier period, foreign journalists were still able to travel round the country and establish personal contacts with Soviet friends. But the purges of the 1930s made most Russians permanently afraid of contacts with foreigners.[12] Moreover, after the onset of the cold war, the Soviet authorities subjected foreigners to further restrictions. They were not allowed to travel more than 40 kilometres (25 miles) outside Moscow without notifying the Soviet Foreign Ministry in advance; and certain areas of the country were declared permanently out of bounds. A law of 1947, still enforced 20 years later, forbade foreign journalists, diplomats or other representatives to make any direct contacts with Soviet institutions or their staff otherwise than through the Foreign Ministry.[13]

It would be quite wrong to give the impression that nothing got better until 1985. In practice, the work of foreign journalists became significantly easier in the post-Stalin era. In the mid-1930s there were no more than about a dozen foreign correspondents in the USSR, but by the end of the 1950s the number had risen to about 150.[14] One substantial improvement from their point of view came in the spring of 1961, when Khrushchev abolished the censorship of outgoing dispatches sent from the USSR by foreign journalists.[15] A further *de facto* improvement came in the 1970s with the rise of detente. The interviewing of Soviet dissidents by foreign journalists, even if theoretically forbidden, was nevertheless tolerated in practice by the Soviet authorities as the price for improving relations with the United States. It remained true, however, that unofficial contact with foreigners involved a substantial degree of risk for Russians.

So far as Soviet media controls are concerned, they have commonly been associated in the public mind with censorship. In actual fact, the traditional system of controls went much wider: they involved not just negative prohibitions, but a whole series of positive injunctions issued to the media in the name of the Communist Party. And, despite considerable variations at different periods of Soviet history, these twin systems of negative censorship and positive propaganda existed continuously from soon after the Bolshevik Revolution down to the late 1980s. The latter – the positive propaganda – is in fact the easier of the two to document from Soviet sources. For example, in 1967 the then head of the Communist Party propaganda department put it this way: 'Every ideological means, whether a book, a play, a film or a radio or television broadcast, must help our struggle for communism.' According to a 1977 article by the then Editor-in-Chief of *Pravda*, Viktor Afanasyev: 'The effectiveness of information work, of ideological activity as a whole, depends on who plans, organizes and controls it; and this is the prerogative of the party.'[16] (Afanasyev retained his editorial post until October 1989.) The same broad principle was reflected, for example, in the statutes of the State Committee on Television and Radio of the USSR, drawn up in 1972 and apparently still unrepealed eighteen years later. They required television and radio editors, among other things, to 'expose bourgeois ideology' and 'to educate Soviet people in a spirit of communist ideological commitment and morality'.[17] In the pre-Gorbachev era, statements such as these were routine. The principle of party control over the media, far from being played down, was repeatedly proclaimed and was one of the axioms of the Soviet system.

Censorship (as distinct from the principle of party control) was rarely mentioned in public in the USSR after the 1930s. The very first Soviet law authorizing censorship was issued two days after the Bolshevik Revolution, on 9 November 1917, and was stated to be temporary. Censorship was, nevertheless, put on a permanent footing by a government decree of 6 June 1922, which set up a so-called 'Main Directorate on Matters of Literature and Publishing', known by the acronym *Glavlit*. The last known law on censorship appeared in 1931.[18] No detailed reference to the subject subsequently appeared until November 1988, when the then head of *Glavlit*, Vladimir Boldyrev, was interviewed in *Izvestiya*.[19] Soviet archives on censorship remain, up to the present time, closed.

Furthermore, many Soviet legal enactments were traditionally classified as 'sub-legal acts',[20] which meant that they did not have to be published.

The system of censorship which the post-1985 Soviet leaders inherited included, in particular, the following four elements:

(1) The *Glavlit* organization (known by then as 'The State Committee for the Preservation of Secrets in the Press'), whose formal sanction was required before anything appeared in print or in the media. *Glavlit* kept a permanent, and regularly updated, list of forbidden topics which almost to the end had prohibited any reference to itself. In theory its function was not that of censorship but simply of protecting secrets. In practice, it exercised its power far more widely: for example, even certain quotations from Lenin were banned. Its powers of preliminary censorship were formally abolished as of 1 August 1990: its functions had been reduced to a mere formality for some time prior to that.[21]

(2) A ban on the unauthorized use of photocopying or other duplicating machinery. The ban had been imposed by an unpublished decree of the USSR Council of Ministers.[22] It was later ruled that all unpublished enactments affecting individual rights were automatically invalidated.

(3) A system of 'closed sections' (*spetskhrany*) in libraries. A Soviet article, published in 1990, on the closed section of the Lenin Library in Moscow reported that 'inaccessible' publications had fallen into four groups: (i) anti-communist books or newspapers published in Russia during the civil war of 1917-21; (ii) material legally published in the USSR between 1918 and 1936 which referred to leaders who had been arrested during the purges; (iii) Russian-language books and newspapers published abroad; and (iv) foreign books and newspapers. From the mid-1970s, the 'closed section' also included writings by recent Soviet émigrés. Some authors (in particular, Trotsky and Solzhenitsyn) had been subject to a 'double prohibition' and could be consulted only with the greatest difficulty. All in all, according to this article, the 'closed section' of the Lenin Library contained over 300,000 book titles, more than 560,000 periodicals and at least a million newspapers.[23]

(4) An elaborate system for the jamming of foreign broadcasts, installed in 1939 and selectively operated between the late 1940s and December 1988. Coordination of jamming in the Moscow area was conducted from the tower of Moscow's Taganka theatre.[24]

Occasionally, though not very often, the reasons for secrecy were touched on by the Soviet authorities. Stalin had said in March 1937 that 'to win a battle, you need several armies. To lose it, only a few spies'.[25] In later years, the secrecy became less paranoid, and was sometimes criticized in public, long before the Gorbachev era.[26] When drawing attention to the scale of past Soviet censorship, it would be incorrect to give the impression of a changeless society consisting only of grey. uniformity until 1985. The stagnation of the Brezhnev era should not be equated with sterility. Despite all its repressive features, it coincided with a notable decline of fear among ordinary Russians. Even at that time a number of new ideas were openly ventilated. For example, the notion of 'pluralism' in relation to public opinion was mentioned in the *Large Soviet Encyclopedia* as far back as 1974.[27] Although such ideas produced few results at the time, their eventual impact was to be revolutionary.

The damage caused to Soviet society by excessive secrecy was emphasized over and over again during the Gorbachev years. What is also worth remembering is the extent to which Soviet secrecy must, at least indirectly, have affected the climate of opinion abroad. A former American ambassador to Moscow in the late 1940s approvingly quoted the saying that 'there are no experts on the Soviet Union; there are only varying degrees of ignorance'.[28] Even in the more open climate of the 1970s, the whole debate in the United States over detente was to a significant extent influenced by the lack of 'normal' information about Soviet military strategy and foreign policy intentions. Doves and hawks in the West might disagree in their interpretation of Soviet policies, but almost everyone agreed that those policies could not be accepted at face value. Such was the legacy of the Soviet past – a legacy which now shows real signs of vanishing.

2
GLASNOST AFTER 1985: ITS ORIGINS AND MEANING

During the years after 1985, many, if not most, Western observers were sceptical about glasnost and were inclined to dismiss it as nothing more than (1) an attempt to strengthen the Soviet system or (2) a largely cosmetic exercise or an exercise in public relations, or even (3) a deliberate attempt to deceive the West. The last of these explanations became very difficult to sustain after the opening of the Berlin Wall. As to the second explanation, it may have had some plausibility. The Soviet media immediately before 1985 had an appalling public relations record. The degree of secrecy (illustrated by the traditional ban on reporting crime or accidents) went far beyond what rational security considerations would have required. Furthermore, the official silences on, for example, the shooting down of the Korean airliner in September 1983 and the last illnesses of Brezhnev, Andropov and Chernenko must have caused acute embarrassment to Soviet diplomats besieged by questions from foreign journalists. Therefore the call for less secrecy may well have attracted support from at least some members of the Soviet establishment who were not liberals.

As to the first possibility, the claim that glasnost was simply an attempt to strengthen the Soviet system is obviously true in a sense – although one can also argue that liberals and conservatives in the Communist Party leadership had radically different ideas as to what kind of a

Soviet system they wanted. The immediate point, however, is that the concept of glasnost was interpreted in totally different ways by different people within the Soviet establishment; and its meaning also differed at different times.

The term itself was never given an official dictionary definition – although a Communist Party resolution 'On glasnost', adopted in July 1988, said that it arose from a public need for 'full and objective information about everything that is going on in society'. Glasnost, so this resolution further noted, was 'a developing process' which, however, must not be used 'to the detriment of the interests of the Soviet state or society'.[1] The term itself was not new. It had been used by dissidents; and also by Brezhnev at least as far back as 1968.[2] The term was later expressly incorporated into the 1977 Soviet Constitution, article 9 of which called for 'the extension of glasnost' as well as 'constant responsiveness to public opinion'.[3] (At that time, the word 'glasnost' was somewhat unclearly rendered into English as 'publicity', which may help to explain why it failed to attract attention.) The important point, however, is that the term had entered the official Soviet vocabulary well before 1985. When Gorbachev began to use it, therefore, no one could accuse him of ideological heresy.

It may next be recalled that Soviet politics from 1985 to 1991 fell roughly into three periods; and in each one of them, glasnost took on a different meaning. Initially, it was seen as an aid to *economic* 'acceleration': that is, as part of a campaign to get the economy out of the doldrums. It was also a weapon in the anti-corruption campaign first launched by Yury Andropov. Thus, in 1985, glasnost still looked like no more than another example of the 'criticism and self-criticism' which all past Soviet leaders, including Stalin, had talked about so often.

In the second phase – and most visibly from the end of 1986, when Andrei Sakharov was released from exile – glasnost was treated as a lever for the *political* reform of the Soviet system within a one-party framework. This phase saw a progressive and very substantial relaxation of censorship, when a growing number of previously taboo subjects were thrown open to discussion. The culmination of pluralism within a one-party framework came in March 1989 with the holding of the first multi-candidate parliamentary elections, which effectively ended the old 'rubber stamp' Supreme Soviet.

Finally, by early 1990 – with the rise of openly secessionist movements in the Baltic and the abolition of the Communist Party's previous monopoly of power under Article 6 of the Soviet Constitution – the idea of 'reform of the system', or what Gorbachev had termed 'socialist pluralism', gave way to the widespread expression of openly anti-communist views in the media. In any case, during the previous year, the concept of glasnost had to a large extent been equated with, or superseded by, the notion of *free speech*.

The stages by which glasnost developed have been described many times. The intellectual origins of Gorbachev's own thinking on the subject are rather less well known, but are important in relation to the question as to whether the new openness represented a strategy or a mere tactic. Gorbachev's views on glasnost can be traced to the time immediately before he came to power. They subsequently evolved dramatically, in a way which became apparent, certainly, by the second half of 1986. Already in December 1984 (i.e. during the last weeks of Konstantin Chernenko's leadership) Gorbachev had described glasnost as 'an integral part of socialist democracy and a norm of all public life', adding that 'extensive, timely and frank information is evidence of trust in people, of respect for ... their ability to interpret events for themselves'.[4] He mentioned glasnost yet again in his acceptance speech on becoming the Communist Party leader on Chernenko's death in March 1985.[5] Later that same month a *Pravda* leading article said that glasnost must be used for, among other things, 'the further improvement of the moral-political . climate in our society'.[6] Then, in a major speech in April, Gorbachev criticized what he described as 'the inability to talk to people in the language of truth' and added: 'It sometimes happens that a man hears one thing, but sees something else in life. The question is a serious one, not only from the educational, but from the political, point of view.'[7]

The question was, in fact, even more fundamental than it might have seemed on the surface. The discrepancy between the then ideology and the observed reality of Soviet society arguably represented the basic flaw in the entire system. Indeed, one American scholar sees this as the key to Gorbachev's entire thinking: that of a 'true-believing communist ... wrestling with the contrast between theory and reality'.[8]

It is difficult, on this evidence, to explain Gorbachev's glasnost as a mere piece of improvisation. However, during his first year in office the top item on the agenda was still economics, not political reform. In the summer of 1986 this was radically to change. It is hard to pinpoint the exact moment when the change occurred – though it seems certain that the Chernobyl disaster on 26 April 1986 was one of the turning-points. The accident was initially detected in Sweden. The first, very brief, Soviet report came only a full two days later. In the meantime the Soviet media began to attack Western reports for alleged exaggeration. Only on 14 May – more than a fortnight after the event – did Gorbachev finally decide to go on Soviet television and elevate the accident to the level of headline news. Meanwhile, the health of millions of people living in the radiated area had been put at risk, since no one had warned them in good time of the need to leave.[9]

The next piece of crucial evidence as to Gorbachev's thinking about glasnost comes from a summary – unofficial but seemingly authentic – of a conversation which he had with a group of Soviet writers on 19 June 1986. It was on this occasion that he insisted on the need to make the process of change irreversible and made the much-quoted remark: 'If we do not, who will? If not now, when?' It was also at this meeting that Gorbachev, apparently for the very first time, identified democratization as the key issue, arguing that this was what the USSR's enemies most feared. ('They are worried by one thing: if democracy develops under us, if that happens, then we will win.') Here for the first time glasnost was presented as one of the key instruments in democratization: 'We don't have an opposition … How then can we monitor ourselves? Only through criticism and self-criticism. And most of all through glasnost.' However, he immediately added a caveat: 'There can be no implementation of democracy without glasnost. But, at the same time, democracy without limits is anarchy. That's why it's complicated.' He was also at that time against delving into the Soviet past: 'If we start trying to deal with the past, we'll lose all our energy. It would be like hitting the people over the head… We'll sort out the past. We'll put everything in its place. But right now we have to direct our energy forward.'[10]

If this account is authentic, it indicates that Gorbachev launched the policy of glasnost for strategic, and certainly not just for tactical, reasons. There is at least one reason why such an explanation makes sense. At that time, Gorbachev's powers stemmed not from the Soviet parliament (as they were later to do), but from the conservative-dominated Communist

Party hierarchy. The party hierarchy was well-placed to obstruct him – or even to depose him, as it had deposed Khrushchev in 1964. In those circumstances, one of the few ways in which Gorbachev *could* put pressure on the conservatives was by relaxing the censorship and releasing information aimed at mobilizing support for reform. It also appears that Gorbachev clearly foresaw – even though he gravely underrated – the risks which openness entailed for the system. His stated goal of 'democracy' without 'anarchy' does help to explain his later political zigzags – which many people saw as pure opportunism. At all events, what seems quite clear is that 'glasnost' as a lever for political reform was originally (in 1986) initiated from above, not from below. Its origins were entirely dissimilar to those which gave rise to the limited reforms in Poland in the late 1970s and early 1980s, after the emergence of the 'Solidarity' movement. In the Polish case, the then leadership was simply reacting to grass-roots demands, as a result of weakness and as part of a defensive, rearguard manoeuvre. But in the Soviet Union in 1986 no comparable mass movement or grass-roots demands had yet materialized. Glasnost at that time was very much a revolution from above.

Soon after this writers' meeting, Gorbachev made a number of public speeches in much the same vein. In a speech delivered in Khabarovsk and broadcast on 31 July, he again emphasized the importance of glasnost in the absence of an opposition, but this apparently proved too sensitive: the reference to the lack of an opposition was deleted from the otherwise verbatim reports of the speech in the Soviet press.[11] The autumn of 1986 saw further significant straws in the wind. In September, plans were published for a major programme of legislation for the next four years, including a new law on referendums, on state security and on 'the press and information' (the latter was originally scheduled for publication in draft in the fourth quarter of 1986).[12] Meanwhile, in October, Gorbachev made another ideological innovation: he declared the priority of 'all-human values' over 'class' values – a clear departure from the traditional Bolshevik view.[13] In November, plans for reform of the administration of justice were announced: they were aimed not only at combating crime but also at preventing 'unwarranted detentions and arrests'.[14] In December, Gorbachev expressly renounced any claim by the Soviet Communist Party to absolute infallibility: he told a Yugoslav communist delegation in Moscow that 'no party possesses a certificate to the absolute truth'.[15]

15

Glasnost after 1985: its origins and meaning

At that time, no political reforms had yet been implemented; but it would have been clear to anyone familiar with the traditional ideology that major doctrinal changes were about to be made. Practical changes were soon to follow: the release of Andrei Sakharov from exile in December; and then, in January 1987, Gorbachev's proposal for an end to one-candidate elections.[16]

The chronology of subsequent political reforms does not concern us. With regard to the origins of glasnost during the Gorbachev era, the evidence would appear to indicate the following:

(1) Glasnost meant different things to different Soviet leaders, and its official meaning radically changed over time.

(2) Gorbachev's own interpretation of the term steadily changed; but one can detect a certain intellectual continuity in his thinking. Even in 1985 he spoke of it as a means of achieving greater honesty and contact with reality. Already by the summer of 1986, he had publicly linked it with the notion of basic political reform.

(3) Glasnost was never *synonymous* with democracy, free speech or political reform. It became important as a possible *bridge* to these things.

(4) Glasnost did not begin as a rearguard manoeuvre by the leadership in response to pressure from below. It was launched quite deliberately from the top (by Gorbachev and his supporters in the Politburo), and was consciously intended to be a lever for change.

(5) The process of change led to unintended results and got out of Gorbachev's control – which is not to say that he necessarily regretted his original choice of glasnost as an instrument of reform.

3

TOWARDS FREEDOM OF INFORMATION: DEVELOPMENTS UP TO 1992

As far back as 1968, the late Academician Andrei Sakharov had specifically called for legislation to guarantee press freedom. 'The situation involving censorship', he wrote, 'is such that it can hardly be corrected for any length of time simply by "liberalized" directives.' He went on to propose the adoption of 'a special law on the press and information that would clearly and convincingly define what can and what cannot be printed and would place the responsibility on competent people who would be under public control'.[1]

It was more than two decades before this proposal was implemented. On 1 August 1990 a Soviet law finally came into force 'On the press and other media of mass information',[2] which set out to fulfil precisely these conditions. This law has now been superseded (on Russian territory) by a law passed on 6 February 1992 'On the media of mass information', which is, in broad outline, similar although more detailed.[3] Of this, more in a moment. Nevertheless, despite the present state of flux, the 1990 law on the media still remains important – as a historical watershed, being the very first enactment of its kind since 1917. However, its passage in the summer of 1990 hardly gave rise to jubilation. It was, in effect, a legal codification in a context of growing legal, political and economic anarchy. The provisions of this law, and the difficulties in which it had to operate, are the subject to which we now turn.

It should first be mentioned, however, that press freedom had by that time already become a *de facto* reality in important ways. Even if censors remained in place in newspaper offices (they formally withdrew at the end of July 1990), they apparently interfered less and less. The intellectual climate had drastically changed: one could argue that the decisive threshold of press freedom was crossed in 1989 with the publication in Moscow of Alexander Solzhenitsyn's *Gulag Archipelago*.[4] Contrary to some predictions, glasnost did not lead to the disappearance of the unofficial *samizdat* press (which had previously been the main vehicle for dissident writings). According to a Soviet book which appeared in 1990, the number of *samizdat* periodicals was about 10 in July 1986, but rose to about 30 in July 1987, to about 100 in July 1988 and 323 a year later.[5]

Media freedom did not become absolute. But the criteria for deciding what could be published radically changed. By 1990 it had become permissible to argue that the 1917 Bolshevik Revolution had been a mistake;[6] and to attack the KGB (as shown by the case of ex-KGB General Oleg Kalugin, who was stripped of his KGB pension after attacking his former employers but who escaped prosecution by virtue of winning a parliamentary by-election to the Supreme Soviet).[7] It had also become permissible to criticize Gorbachev, the President, and call for his resignation.[8] On the other hand, certain taboos remained. There was, for instance, very little press criticism of events in China following the massacre on Tiananmen Square in 1989. There had been virtually no criticism of the former communist regimes in Eastern Europe prior to their collapse in 1989. The reporting of events in areas of unrest such as Nagorny Karabakh had been patchy. Furthermore, Boris Yeltsin had not had easy access to television prior to his election as President of the Russian Parliament in May 1990.[9] According to a senior Communist Party official interviewed in *Pravda* in that year, the main guideline for what should be published was not 'the interests of the party', but the interests of 'civil peace'.[10]

The 1990 media law
Even today, after the demise of the Soviet Union, the 1990 law has to be seen as a legal benchmark, because it broke new ground in several respects. It effectively legitimized the expression of anti-communist opinions. It created some of the preconditions for genuine media inde-

pendence. Last but not least, it gave a role to the courts in settling disputes over the law's interpretation.

The law (which applied to what were called 'information media': i.e. films, radio and television as well as newspapers and periodicals, but apparently not to books) ran to seven chapters and was far more precise than any previous Soviet enactment on the subject. Article 1 forbade censorship. The only limits on free expression were those laid down in Article 5, which forbade: the disclosure of state or other legally protected secrets, appeals for the overthrow or alteration by force of the existing state or social system, the propaganda of war, violence, or racial, national or religious intolerance, the spreading of pornography or the use of the media for the purpose of committing acts criminally punishable by law. Article 5 also contained safeguards against the defamation of individuals or invasion of their privacy.

The second part of the law laid it down that newspapers (or broadcasting stations or other 'information media', as the case might be) could be founded not only by organizations but by individual Soviet citizens aged over 18 (Article 7). One of the law's central provisions was that 'information media' had as a rule to be registered, with a specified local or All-Union authority (Article 8). However, registration was not required in the case of material intended for private circulation only, or in the case of publications with a print-run of fewer than 1,000 copies (Article 10). This exemption was of great importance, because it effectively decriminalized *samizdat*. Registration, i.e. permission to publish, could be refused on only certain specified grounds, in particular (1) that the title or editorial aims of the publication appeared to run counter to the restrictions on free expression laid down in Article 5 (and summarized above); and (2) that another publication had already been registered under the same name (Article 11).

A publication or 'information medium' could be closed down against its will where it had, for the second time within a year, contravened the restrictions on free expression in Article 5 as stated above. Registration could be withdrawn either by the registering authority or by the court (Article 13). However, there was a right of appeal to a court against either a refusal to register a publication or a decision to close it down (Article 14). This was the first time in Soviet legal history that the courts had been given such an autonomous power with regard to the media. The illegal publication of unregistered material could be punished by a fine of up to 500 roubles,* imposed by a court, together with the destruction of the print-run. A repetition of the offence could be punished by a fine of up to 1,000 roubles and by confiscation of the offender's printing press or other equipment (Article 37). Imprisonment, however, was not one of the penalties.

The 1990 media law also broke new ground in setting out to provide a legal framework for the relations between founders of publications, editors and journalists (Article 15). These could be regulated by a set of rules, to be approved at a general meeting of the journalists concerned (Article 16). The individual journalist had certain duties, for example that of checking the accuracy of his (or her) information (Article 32). He was required (in common with his editor) to protect the sources of confidential information – except where ordered by a court to disclose them (Article 28). He was also given certain new rights – in particular, he could refuse to sign any material 'which in his opinion had been distorted in the process of being edited' (Article 30). In view of the pre-1985 record of the Soviet media, this right was far from trivial.

Article 26 of the 1990 law gave individuals or organizations the further right to reply to inaccurate information which represented 'a slur on their honour and dignity'. If their replies or corrections were not published within a month, the offender could be sued in court (Article 27). One of the earliest test cases of this rule was a court action brought by a member of the Congress of People's Deputies, Galina Starovoitova, against *Pravda* and TASS. She sued them for falsely reporting that she had advocated 'physical reprisals' against political opponents. On 4 February 1991 a Moscow court found in her favour and ordered the defendants to apologize. It appears that they did not do so. Nevertheless, successful litigation in a Soviet court against *Pravda* and TASS was something entirely new.[11]

Of particular importance to our theme are the international aspects of this law. Article 33 expressly gave Soviet citizens 'a right of access to information from foreign sources, including direct television broadcasting, radio and the press'. This appeared to make the jamming of foreign stations illegal and was a complete reversal of earlier Soviet policy. The

*In 1990 this was equivalent to between one and two months' average salary in the USSR.

same article stated that international cooperation relating to mass information was to be governed by international treaties which would override
this particular law. Under Article 34, the status of foreign journalists in
the Soviet Union as well as the activities of foreign diplomats relating to
information were to be governed by Soviet laws which had to be in
accordance with international treaties. The apparent result was that
foreign journalists in the USSR were given legally enforceable rights
when carrying out their professional activities.

The 1990 media law was, certainly until the coup of August 1991, the
main statute governing freedom of expression.[12] From a legal point of
view it contained one obvious gap. For although Article 5 forbade the
disclosure of state or other secrets, it did not specify what constituted a
state secret. This legal gap still remains unremedied as of early 1992.
Another possible loophole in the new law lay in the various emergency
powers which the authorities then possessed and which conferred the
right, in certain circumstances, to impose media controls. However, with
the demise of the USSR these powers have, of course, vanished.

The 1992 media law

Before discussing the problems which surrounded the 1990 law, we shall
briefly move forward and compare it with its successor – the Russian
media law of 1992, which is now in operation. The two laws are very
similar in their broad outlines, although different in detail and somewhat
differently arranged. (Both were originally drafted by the same authors.[13])
Thus the Russian law forbids censorship; but goes further than its 1990
predecessor in specifically forbidding the setting up or financing of any
agencies whose tasks include media censorship (Article 3). The restrictions on free expression are almost, but not quite, the same as those of the
1990 law (1992 law, Article 4).[14] Newspapers and other media can be
closed down only by their founder; or by a court, in cases where they
have repeatedly during the previous twelve months overstepped the
permitted limits of free expression as just defined, and have been officially warned about this in writing (*Ibid.*, Article 16). Like the 1990 law,
its Russian replacement lays down a procedure for the registration of
newspapers or other 'media' (Articles 8-15). Here again, however, there
are a number of exemptions and there is no need to register publications

21

with a print-run of less than 1,000 copies (Article 12). The grounds for refusing registration (set out in Article 13) are substantially the same as in the 1990 law summarized above; and in the event of refusal, the applicant can appeal to the courts (Article 61(1)).

The 1992 law also follows the law of 1990 in providing that the relations between founders, editors and journalists can be established by rules approved at a general meeting of the journalistic staff concerned (Article 20). It maintains the principle, among others, that editors may not disclose the source of confidential information which has been obtained on condition that the source is to be kept confidential – except where a court orders otherwise (Article 41). As before, journalists remain under a duty to check the accuracy of their information (Article 49(2)); and they retain the right to refuse to sign material which they consider to have been distorted in the process of editing (Article 47(11)). The law provides a detailed procedure enabling individuals or organizations to reply to inaccurate information about them in the media (Articles 43-46). Any damage caused to them as a result can be the subject of compensation, to be fixed by the courts (Article 62). Unlike its predecessor, the present law does not lay down fines or other specific penalties for those who offend against it. It merely states that breaches entail 'criminal, administrative, · disciplinary or other liability' under Russian law (Articles 58-60).

In certain ways, however, the 1992 law does cover new ground. It envisages the setting up of a 'Federal Commission for Television and Radio', to be responsible for granting franchises to private broadcasting stations. The conditions for the granting of these franchises are not stated (there is no reference to any obligation to maintain impartiality in news coverage); but the franchises may be awarded through competition and may be withdrawn in certain circumstances (Articles 30-32). The new law also imposes a number of controls on pornography.[15]

With regard to relations with the outside world, the 1992 law is more detailed, but slightly more restrictive than that of 1990. Thus Article 7 of the new law imposes a clear restriction on foreign control of the Russian media: it provides that the citizen of another state or a stateless person not permanently resident in Russia is disqualified from being the founder of a newspaper or other mass information medium. Article 54 reaffirms the right of Russian citizens to receive information from the foreign media. Direct television broadcasts from abroad must not be interfered with except in accordance with any international treaties which Russia may enter into. The same article also lays down that the distribution in Russia of publications controlled and financed from abroad and not registered under this law requires the permission of the Russian Ministry of the Press and Information, unless otherwise provided by treaty. Article 55 recognizes the journalistic status of accredited foreign correspondents, but appears to insist on reciprocity: it allows the Russian government to impose restrictions on journalists from countries which impose restrictions on Russian journalists.

Media freedom in practice since 1990

It is of course rather too early to assess the impact of this latest legislation. But the experience of the period since August 1990 is still of some importance. The 1990 media law was itself affected by a number of developments – some, but not all, of which have now passed into history. The conflict between Yeltsin and Gorbachev, the crisis in the Baltic in January 1991, and the start of the disintegration of the Soviet Union all produced a severe strain on the media. The main casualty, however, was not the press, but Soviet television (then headed by Leonid Kravchenko, a Gorbachev appointee, who imposed tight editorial controls and was sacked following the coup for cooperating with the plotters). Complaints that television freedom was being curtailed reached a peak after the shootings in Vilnius on 13 January 1991. On that day and for some time afterwards, the main Moscow television news programme, *Vremya*, reported that Soviet troops had not been the first to open fire. This gave rise · to accusations of downright lying, since it flatly contradicted the evidence of foreign journalists on the spot. Gorbachev himself appeared to support the official version of the shootings when he spoke to the Supreme Soviet on 14 January; and again two days later when he made a suggestion (which he almost at once withdrew) that the 1990 media law should be suspended. In the end it was agreed that the law's operation should be referred to the Supreme Soviet committee responsible for glasnost, and nothing much happened.[16]

The Soviet media were also affected at this time by the conflict between Gorbachev and Yeltsin – whom the Russian parliament had elected as its chairman on 29 May 1990. Yeltsin's election was followed by what came to be known as a 'war of laws' between the two leaders, in which the Russian republic declared that its laws took precedence over those of the USSR. This led, among other things, to disputes relating to the press. Thus in the autumn of 1990 the Russian republican leaders complained that they were being allocated less than 4 per cent of the paper produced on their territory; and the Russian parliament passed a resolution asserting direct control over such paper, and taking control away from the centre.[17]

The most serious dispute in 1990-91 where the media were concerned centred on whether the Russian republic should be allowed its own independent radio and television channels. (Other republics already had their own broadcasting channels – over which Moscow had effectively lost control.) The dispute dragged on for several months. The Russian republic got its own radio station – Radio Rossiya – on 10 December 1990, and although its transmitters were relatively weak it claimed an audience of 30 million listeners. During the Baltic crisis it put out its own reports, which often flatly contradicted the official Soviet version of events. Russian television began to broadcast only later: the delay was apparently due to Gorbachev's initial opposition. However, he eventually gave way; and, on 13 May 1991, Russia's television channel was at last launched.[18] It comprised a 6½-hour daily programme, including a news bulletin whose political slant differed markedly from that of All-Union Soviet television.

The conflicts just outlined are, of course, a matter of history, now that the Soviet Union has broken up. But the period from 1990 to 1991 also highlighted other questions facing the media, which are unlikely to go away so quickly. The most serious issues concern, first, the transition to the market; and second, the disposal of the property of the now dissolved Soviet Communist Party.

The transition of the press to market principles effectively began on 1 January 1991; and it gave rise to one of the gravest difficulties which the uncensored media had yet had to face. The price of newsprint began to rise steeply[19] and has continued to do so. The same was true of postal charges, which were said to have been unaltered since 1939.[20] For the very first time in living memory, Soviet readers had to do without Sunday newspapers. The prices of *Pravda* and *Izvestiya* doubled, having been virtually unchanged since the 1920s. From the start of 1991 the newsprint allocation and print-run of a newspaper depended on the scale of readers' subscriptions. In this new atmosphere of competition, communist publications began to lose out and independent ones gained. Thus the print-run of *Pravda* fell steeply (from 7,700,000 in December 1990 to 3,120,000 in the following January; by early 1992 it had dropped to 1,385,000). By contrast the now much more radical *Komsomol'skaya pravda*, which operated from the same building, had a print-run in early 1991 of over 18 million copies. However, even the independent press sometimes suffered. The popular weekly *Argumenty i fakty* had to quadruple its price; and, because of the ensuing loss of readers, it had to reduce its print-run from over 33 million copies in 1990 to just over 24 million in 1991. The paper remarked that 'in exchange for the censorship which has vanished into the past, economic sanctions have arrived'.[21]

These 'economic sanctions' show no sign of coming to an end: the freeing of prices on 2 January 1992 raised fears of widespread newspaper bankruptcies. The most immediate threat came from the further drastic rise in postal charges and in the cost of newsprint – which still remain under government control and have not been privatized. The now independent *Komsomol'skaya pravda* even talked of the press in the former USSR being on the brink of 'an information catastrophe'.[22] Meanwhile, in January 1992, the Russian government said that it was planning to allocate 7 milliard roubles to assist the press – including such anti-government newspapers as *Pravda*.[23] Not everyone, however, found this reassuring. A few days later, a senior Russian television editor, Eduard Sagalayev, made a speech to an American audience in Atlanta, Georgia, in which he accused the Russian authorities of trying to exert 'financial leverage on those media which dare to criticize the government'.[24] Whether justified or not, such fears undoubtedly exist.

The second issue still to be resolved – the disposal of the Communist Party's assets – was already being hotly debated in the autumn of 1990. One of the main complaints of the then anti-communist opposition about the media legislation of 1990 was that despite its guarantees of free expression it left the ownership of media facilities largely in the Communist Party's hands. At that time, it was the anti-communists who complained about the government having an economic leverage over the media.

Communist Party control over the media had been axiomatic until·

1990. The party itself (at its last congress in July 1990) was said to own 114 publishing houses; and to provide printing facilities for 406 newspapers and 286 journals.[25] That seemed to be an understatement, because the party had up till then controlled almost all the thousands of newspapers throughout the country, and the question of whether it actually owned them had sometimes been undefined. The value of the party's undoubtedly huge assets was semi-officially estimated at 4 billion roubles in August 1991.[26] But quite apart from the question of fraudulent concealment (notably by sending money abroad), valuation of assets is likely to be difficult. One can only guess what the buildings or their contents would fetch on a hypothetical open market, assuming there were buyers. In fact, the question was settled by government action. The Communist Party – which was suspended in Russia just after the coup and banned in the following November – has now been deprived of its assets.[27]

Immediately after the coup, on 23 August 1991, Yeltsin issued a decree suspending *Pravda* and five other newspapers accused of supporting the coup. The decree was cancelled on 10 September, but the Communist Party press is a thing of the past. *Pravda*, on the initiative of its staff, was re-registered under the 1990 media law as an independent newspaper: it came back onto the streets on 31 August after a gap of only eight days. Other party newspapers have re-registered in a similar way, under non-communist auspices. However, *Pravda* in particular ceased to own the premises from which it operated[28] and ran into debt. The news, on 13 March 1992, that the paper was suspending publication hardly came as a surprise. The party publishing houses have now to all intents and purposes been placed under the control of the post-coup Russian leadership, which therefore wields an enormous power over the media, in fact if not in law. It remains to be seen whether they are parcelled out among newspapers of genuinely different points of view. But the manner in which the party's publishing houses are disposed of will clearly be a crucial factor in deciding whether Russia gets a genuinely pluralistic press in the years ahead.

Pressures to maintain legal restrictions on the media have continued even in the post-communist era. This was shown by some of the attempts to whittle down the 1992 media law. In December 1991, for example, the Russian parliament passed an amendment which would have required journalists to disclose their sources not only to the courts (as provided by the 1990 law) but to legal investigators. Another amendment would have forbidden the making of film or recordings without the consent of all participants (which could, somewhat absurdly, have outlawed the filming of crowds or meetings). Boris Yeltsin then threatened to veto these changes, which were shortly afterwards withdrawn.[29]

The immediate future for the Russian media therefore seems bleak. Yet as regards the recent past, it could probably be claimed that Russia, following the passage of the media law in 1990, made more progress towards press freedom than it had ever done in its history. Preliminary press censorship really did vanish (as this writer himself heard from journalists in Moscow). Even after the Baltic crisis of 1991 the Russian press remained remarkably outspoken: several newspapers, including the influential *Literaturnaya gazeta* and the *Moscow News*, published forthright condemnations of the shootings in Vilnius.[30] There were frequent complaints that Soviet television, in particular, was being censored; but the Soviet press was one of the principal sources of these complaints.[31] It was all very far removed from the earlier 'totalitarian' stereotype – in which the media not only were forbidden to criticize government policy but were under a positive duty to praise it. Even during the August coup itself, the plotters did not have it all their own way in the press: *Pravda*, for example, contained an item on 20 August which referred to Yeltsin's call for a general strike; and *Izvestiya* on the same day printed an extra edition with extensive reporting of the opposition to the coup. And taking 1991 as a whole, the press was probably more diverse than at any previous time, except possibly for the months after February 1917. Publications covering a whole spectrum of views, from anti-communist to hardline communist, were freely on sale – as were a whole number of others, including those of anti-semites and astrologers. Television had a less smooth passage, but even here, there were remarkable signs of journalistic freedom.

At the present time the Russian media are not surprisingly undergoing rapid changes and are in a state of some flux. But it should be noted that much of the groundwork for press freedom had been laid well before 1991. Needless to say, the main threat to the media, and indeed to Russian society as a whole, comes not from local difficulties but from the danger of total economic collapse.

It only remains, finally, to mention a problem which Soviet or Russian legislators may have failed to address. They might arguably have done better, both in 1990 and in 1992, to pass entirely separate laws for broadcasting and the press, rather than a single law for both. Broadcasting, in contrast to the press, is subject in all countries to a degree of state regulation, and is usually required to maintain a certain degree of political impartiality. This is itself far from easy to define, let alone practise. And it should be noted, where Russia is concerned, that over the past seven decades the very notion of impartiality has been not only disregarded but vehemently denied, for philosophical and ideological reasons. Until the late 1980s, the official Soviet injunction to journalists had been that of so-called 'party-mindedness' (*partiinost'*), i.e. dedication to the communist cause; and it had been said, for instance, that 'party-mindedness and objectivity in communist journalism are inseparable'.[32] According to the traditional Soviet view, both communists and anti-communists engaged in propaganda – with the sole difference that Soviet communicators openly admitted what they were doing. It must be recognized in all fairness that television in the USSR had begun to show signs of pluralism, certainly by 1990. But the traditional disbelief in impartiality is unlikely to vanish overnight in a post-communist Russia, especially if Russian society becomes polarized as a result of crisis. Impartiality in broadcasting is a subject which frequently gives rise to disagreement even in Britain. For Russian journalists, it is likely be be an especially formidable challenge.

4

COMMUNICATION ACROSS FRONTIERS: PROGRESS SO FAR

Already by 1990, the Soviet Union had become more open to the outside world than at any time since 1917, or indeed ever before. This was mainly the result of changes in Soviet policy after 1985. But it was also the product of other, more long-term, factors. The post-Stalin era had seen a slow, but nevertheless significant, incremental expansion of East-West contacts, which in some ways had prepared the ground for the later radical reforms. Another change, which had nothing directly to do with the cold war, was the development, worldwide, of communications technology. Western broadcasts to the Soviet Union had won a substantial audience, certainly by the 1970s – even though unwelcome to the country's then leaders. Technological innovations, ranging from the mass production of tape-recorders to the development of transnational television, had done much to undermine the regime's monopoly of information.

Relaxation of cross-border communications under Gorbachev

Openness to information from abroad
The Soviet Union's new openness to opinions from abroad became discernible at least by 1987. At the end of March in that year, Mrs Thatcher was able during a visit to Moscow to set out her views at length and without censorship in a long interview on Soviet television.[1] In October 1987, during a live television link-up by satellite between Moscow

and Washington, Senator Daniel Moynihan was able to inform his Soviet audience that they lived in a 'human rights hell' where restrictions on emigration and press freedom were worse than those imposed under the tsars. The programme was seen by an estimated 150 million Soviet viewers.[2] By 1991 (and indeed before that), the views of the critics of the Soviet system were not merely tolerated but in many cases were being actively solicited. Thus in April 1991, the Moscow *Literaturnaya gazeta* devoted an entire page to the work of Amnesty International and its specific proposals for improving human rights in the USSR; and in the following month Amnesty International was authorized to open an office in Moscow.[3] Examples of similar openness to the outside world could be enormously extended: it might incidentally be mentioned that in 1991 a new publication appeared in Moscow, under the title 'Radio Digest', which devotes itself specifically to reproducing the contents of foreign broadcasts.[4]

Western views therefore get direct access to the Russian media, just as Russian views get media coverage in the West. Even before the August coup, the ending of domestic censorship had clearly rendered obsolete the traditional ban on the import of anti-communist literature from abroad, because such literature would no longer have been illegal if published in the USSR. Another liberalizing measure was the decision, with effect from 15 August 1989, to introduce 'red' and 'green' customs channels at Moscow's Sheremetyevo airport, which meant that travellers from abroad with nothing to declare could now go through the customs without having their luggage searched.[5]

Yet another result of this liberalization was, of course, the total ending of the Soviet jamming of Western broadcasts which had begun in the late 1940s and had continued in one form or another throughout the cold war years. Here, the first signs of a changed Soviet policy came during the Reykjavik summit in October 1986, when Gorbachev proposed that the Soviet Union would stop jamming the radio station Voice of America in return for American help in setting up a Soviet radio transmitter in or near US territory which could reach an American audience directly. (A few days later Gorbachev mentioned his idea in a Soviet television broadcast which was published in *Pravda*. It seems to have been the first time that the word 'jamming'- *glushenie* – had appeared in print in a Soviet newspaper.[6])

In the event, Moscow dropped its demand for reciprocity. In 1987, it ended the jamming of the BBC and Voice of America; and in the following year it also stopped jamming the Munich-based Radio Liberty (which, unlike the other two stations, had been jammed without interruption since its foundation in 1950).[7] Intermittent Soviet media attacks on these stations continued for some time. Nevertheless the situation by 1989-90 was basically different from what it had been in the pre-Gorbachev period, when jamming was switched on or off purely at the discretion of the authorities. Foreign stations broadcasting in Russian or other languages of the USSR became perfectly free to work inside the country. Soviet citizens (as distinct from émigrés) were by then willing quite openly to give interviews to these stations, which they seldom had been before.

In March 1989, *Pravda* for the very first time published an article on the jamming operation (which had been run by a secret department of the Soviet Ministry of Communications, set up 50 years earlier and now said to have been totally abolished).[8] The very appearance of this article seemed to indicate an intention to make the abolition of jamming irreversible. Article 33 of the 1990 media law and Article 54 of the 1992 law appeared to make jamming unlawful, since, as already mentioned in Chapter 3, it gave citizens the right of access to information through foreign sources, including direct television broadcasts, radio broadcasts and the press.

Freedom of travel

Of course Soviet censorship was never the only Western complaint against the USSR, where East-West contacts were concerned. Ever since the 1970s, one of the main bones of East-West contention had concerned the movement of people across frontiers. From 1975 onwards, the United States was barred by statute (under the Jackson-Vanik amendment to the Trade Act of that year) from granting Most Favoured Nation status to any communist country which refused to allow free emigration.[9] Only in May 1991 did the Soviet Parliament finally adopt a law allowing the emigration of its citizens as of right. Of this, more in a moment. But it may first be pointed out that foreign travel by Soviet citizens, as well as travel by foreigners into the USSR, had by slow degrees been expanding for some years. Soviet emigration had already drastically accelerated. In August 1990, it was stated that out of the 816,000 Soviet citizens who had left their country for good since the Second World War, as many as 344,000 (i.e. 42 per cent of the total) had left in 1988 and 1989.[10]

Table 4.1   Outbound travel from the Soviet Union, 1981–9, in millions

	1981	1982	1983	1984	1985	1986	1987	1988	1989
Total	2.31	2.60	2.77	2.64	2.80	2.99	3.44	4.24	8.00
Of which: to socialist states	1.42	1.53	1.57	1.57	1.74	1.76	2.05	2.74	6.15
to non-socialist states	0.89	1.06	1.20	1.07	1.04	1.23	1.39	1.50	1.71

Note: Figures have been rounded, therefore the totals do not in all cases precisely tally.

Table 4.2   Outbound travel from Soviet Union by destination and purpose of visit, 1989, in thousands

	Total	Tourism	Business	Private	Transport staff
Total	8009*	1650	1114	3640	1605*
Of which:					
to socialist states	6158	1499	712	3249	698
to non-socialist states	1717	151	402	391	773
Including:					
US	82	3	19	46	14
UK	52	2	12	4	34
France	61	3	19	13	26
W. Germany	234	9	47	130	48
Finland	224	57	35	58	74
Israel	41	0	1	40	0

Note: The totals marked with an asterisk include 134,000 personnel who travelled abroad with the Soviet fishing fleet, on scientific expeditions, etc.

Already by the late 1980s, short-term foreign journeys by Soviet citizens had become a little easier. The requirement that all who went abroad required testimonials of political reliability was discontinued.[11] In November 1989, the right to issue foreign passports to those travelling abroad on business was devolved and was no longer the prerogative of the Foreign Ministry.[12] Visa-free trips were sometimes allowed – for example between Finland and Talinn or Leningrad.[13]

Table 4.3   Foreign visitor arrivals in the Soviet Union 1981–9, in millions

	1981	1982	1983	1984	1985	1986	1987	1988	1989
Total	3.46	3.46	4.13	4.19	4.33	4.31	5.24	6.00	7.75*
From socialist states	1.58	1.59	2.36	2.67	2.71	2.71	3.24	4.00	5.59
From non-socialist states	1.70	1.60	1.50	1.30	1.40	1.60	2.00	2.00	2.15

*The 1989 total includes 6,000 stateless individuals who visited the USSR in that year. Figures have been rounded, therefore the totals do not in all cases precisely tally.

Table 4.4   Foreign visitor arrivals in the Soviet Union from selected countries by purpose of visit, 1989, in thousands

	Total	Tourism	Business	Private	Transport staff
US	180	121	48	5	6
UK	89	50	23	1	15
France	82	46	26	2	8
West Germany	234	153	57	10	14
Finland	685	508	98	9	70
Israel	10	2	2	6	0

Sources[14]: Eva Kerpel, *Tourism in Eastern Europe and the Soviet Union: Prospects for Growth and New Market Opportunities* (London: The Economist Intelligence Unit, 1990), pp. 130, 136-7; *Narodnoye Khozyaistvo SSSR v 1989 godu* (Moscow: Goskomstat, 1990), pp. 671-4.

Official figures for Soviet citizens going abroad, and of foreigners visiting the USSR, have now become more freely available. They indicate a gradual increase of movement across borders over quite a long period. Thus, whereas over half a million Soviet citizens were said to have gone abroad in 1956, the figure for 1976 had risen to between 2.6 and 3 million (in 1975-6 some 40 per cent of Soviet travellers abroad were said to have visited non-communist countries).[15] From the 1980s, more detailed breakdowns are available, as shown in Tables 4.1 to 4.4.

The Soviet growth in this area was therefore significant, even though the USSR lagged greatly behind Western countries. It may be noted for the sake of comparison that the number of Americans or American residents travelling abroad was just over 8 million in 1981 and 13.7 million in 1987, the last year for which final figures are available. The number of foreign travellers into the United States in these two years was, respectively, 9 million and 10.4 million.[16] However, even in the pre-Gorbachev period, the USSR was by no means a totally closed society; and by 1989 the amount of cross-border travel was significantly increasing.

Freedom of emigration for Soviet citizens
This, however, did nothing to assuage a bitter and widespread sense of grievance among Soviet citizens, who had not – throughout Soviet history – been entitled as of right either to go abroad or to possess foreign passports. In March 1990, the then editor of the influential *Literaturnaya gazeta*, Fyodor Burlatsky, insisted that the liberalization of the past few years had affected 'only an insignificant number of citizens', such as Jews and other ethnic minorities, or those with relatives abroad; and that, 'for the rest, nearly everything is as before'.[17]

This state of affairs was, however, radically changed under a new law 'On the procedure for exit from the USSR and entry into the USSR', which was passed by the Supreme Soviet on 20 May 1991 and had been due to come into full effect on 1 January 1993.[18] It did away with the requirement that a Soviet citizen must, in order to get a foreign passport, produce an invitation from a foreign host. Under this law a citizen would as a rule be automatically entitled to a foreign passport – which could be refused only temporarily and in specified cases: for example, if the applicant was in possession of state secrets or had contracted not to go abroad, or was under criminal investigation or serving a sentence for a crime. Those wishing to live permanently abroad did not forfeit their citizenship: i.e., they were no longer to be treated as political émigrés.

The implications of this law for civil liberties were even greater than those of the 1990 law on the media. But the most serious problem – with this or any other Russian law on emigration – is certain to be economic rather than legal. There is a real possibility that freedom of travel from the former USSR could accelerate a brain-drain of the country's most skilled scientists, which it could ill afford.[19] The country's acute shortage of foreign currency is almost certain to restrict foreign travel by its citizens for pleasure. And any large-scale emigration is virtually bound to result in immigration curbs being imposed on the Western side. There is as yet no reliable way of knowing how great that emigration will be (estimates of 7 million people wanting to leave for the West have been dismissed as exaggerated).[20] But the unexpected collapse of the Iron Curtain has placed a host of economic problems on the international agenda.

Technological innovations and their influence

Soviet openness to the outside world is not, of course, merely the product of Soviet political change. Recent decades have seen a communications and technological revolution on a worldwide scale which had nothing to do with Soviet politics. One of the best-known examples of this trend – which goes somewhat beyond the scope of our subject – was of course the computer revolution. It would certainly have had an impact on Soviet politics sooner or later even if the Gorbachev reforms had never been launched, because it would have placed the regime in the dilemma of either doing without such technology and being unable to compete with its rivals, or of using it and therefore losing some of its control over the spreading of information.[21] Quite apart from this, however, the channels of communication in the USSR had been changing in important ways for quite some time. The overall effect of the changes was to demonopolize the control of information. And for this very reason the changes were having a noticeable effect on Soviet society well before 1985.

Foreign broadcasting to the USSR is the best-known example. It has been estimated that in 1950, perhaps no more than 8 per cent of Soviet listeners had radio sets capable of tuning into foreign broadcasts.[22] But by 1982, according to a Soviet author, some 40 million short-wave radio sets existed in the country – enough in itself to create a mass audience for foreign radio.[23] (The growth and impact of foreign broadcasting to the former USSR is a subject to which we shall return in Chapters 6 and 7.)

Tape recorders, as a means of circulating ideas, are far less well-known than the radio. Nevertheless they became important in the USSR, certainly from the 1970s onwards. Unlike printing or photocopying equipment, they were never subject to restrictions in the Soviet Union and were sold without hindrance. They became an important vehicle for disseminating music, which the then Soviet authorities were not prepared to broadcast. A Soviet survey quoted in 1985 found that as many as 63 per cent of young people of Komsomol age (i.e. eligible to join the Young Communist League) were in the habit of making musical recordings.[24] Another survey, quoted two years later, found that in Moscow 97 per cent of schoolchildren listened to pop or rock music.[25] A Soviet history textbook for schools, published in Moscow in 1990, made a point of singling out what it called 'the tape-recorder revolution' of the 1960s and 1970s: 'Recordings of songs and also of satirical speeches were copied within the home; they were in practice not amenable to control and they acquired a mass circulation. Although officially unrecognized, they became a part of everyday life and influenced the minds of millions of people.'[26]

Videorecorders are a much newer phenomenon in the USSR, but are very much a growth industry. Certainly by the early 1980s they were appearing on the Soviet black market and were causing visible concern to the then Soviet authorities – as shown by a series of prosecutions for circulating 'pornography' and for engaging in 'speculation'.[27] In 1990, according to one Western estimate, there were no more than 300,000 videorecorders in the country.[28] This may be compared with the figure for the United Kingdom, where in 1990 some 13,889,000 homes had videorecorders; the comparable figure for France was 5,160,000.[29] However, Soviet production of videorecorders has risen dramatically. Prior to 1984, they were not produced in the USSR at all; in 1985, 6,800 were produced; and in 1989 the figure was 125,000.[30]

Domestic television was another technological innovation which helped to erode the old system of controls – and it underwent a huge expansion in the Soviet Union as elsewhere. In 1960 no more than 5 per cent of the Soviet population could watch television, whereas by 1986 no less than 93 per cent were able to do so.[31] This expansion reflected a deliberate policy of successive Soviet leaders who had believed it would enhance the power of official propaganda. In practice, television often had the opposite effect – because the Soviet citizen, once he was able to watch television at home, became more critical and became less and less keen on attending political meetings. Already in the 1970s, Soviet propaganda specialists were noting how the effectiveness of party speakers at gatherings was being undermined by competition from the television screen, because the speakers were unable to convey much information which their audiences had not already heard.[32]

Transnational television, including in some cases direct broadcasting by satellite, is a logical extension of all this; and although its development lies in the future, it has risen unmistakably, and could have enormous long-term consequences for all countries and not just for the former USSR. Direct television broadcasting, by satellite in particular, can have a strong impact on audiences, is difficult to stop and could therefore seriously weaken any media control by a national government. The best-known example to date of transnational television winning a mass audience was that of the former GDR – where domestic television was far less popular than the programmes from West Germany.

This case, although unusual, was not entirely unique. Long before 1985, foreign television had been watched by Soviet viewers in certain border areas. Finnish television has for many years had an audience in parts of Estonia (the two languages are related); and a Soviet book of 1986 reported that foreign programmes were watched not only in the Baltic but also in the Caucasus, Central Asia and the Far East.[33] Certainly since the 1960s, Soviet propaganda specialists had been aware of, and sometimes alarmed by, the prospect of uncontrolled television across frontiers. Thus in 1966 a Soviet sociologist had predicted that this problem would arise 'in the very near future' and added: 'I am not convinced that our Soviet television programmes, in the form in which they exist today, will withstand direct competition from other programmes.'[34]

The Brezhnev leadership was particularly alarmed by the prospect of foreign television broadcasts beamed by satellite into the Soviet Union. In August 1972, the Soviet government went so far as to submit to the UN a draft convention which would have allowed direct satellite television broadcasts by one country to another 'only with the express consent of the latter'. The draft convention would also have required all such broadcasts to be under the control of a government and would have made it legal for a target country to jam such broadcasts.[35]

In the world as a whole, the late 1980s and early 1990s saw notable advances for transnational television, whether relayed by cable (as happens most often) or through direct broadcasting by satellite (DBS). In Europe, the ownership of dish aerials, which can pick up satellite television broadcasts, is still very uneven. In 1990 there were reported to be 1.3

million dish aerials in the United Kingdom as opposed to no more than an estimated 650 in the USSR (though the number is no doubt rapidly increasing). In Poland the number may have reached a remarkable 100,000, while in France it was no more than 40,000.[36]

1991 also saw the launching of the very first television programmes on the World Service of the BBC: to Europe on 11 March and to Asia from 14 October. Its news programme is already rebroadcast on national television in Poland, Czechoslovakia, Hungary, Romania and Yugoslavia. The range of its programmes for Asia will extend from the Black Sea to the Yellow Sea.[37] Meanwhile, a 'Euronews' multilingual satellite television news programme, backed by the EC Commission and by 28 European countries, is due to start broadcasting on 1 January 1993.[38] The growing importance of transnational television had already been underlined by the role of Cable News Network during the Gulf war, and by the fact that CNN was watched in Moscow in 1991, particularly during the attempted coup, a topic to which we shall return in Chapter 6. Russian newspapers are, indeed, already carrying advertisements for the sale of dish aerials, to enable their readers to watch foreign programmes by satellite.[39] Indeed, it was reported that during the autumn of 1991, as many as one in seven Russians were regularly watching Western television programmes, either on their own television media or by satellite.[40] It may also be mentioned that in early 1991 Moscow radio reported tentative plans for a worldwide Soviet television programme in English. Later in the year it was stated that talks were being held on setting up an international television station in St Petersburg to broadcast to Europe.[41]

One naturally cannot know how long it will be before transnational television becomes a mass phenomenon. But its gradual expansion is bound to have at least one result. It will become increasingly difficult for governments to control the influx of information and ideas from abroad. The report on the financing of the BBC, chaired by Professor Alan Peacock and published in 1986, made precisely this point. It contained the following warning:

> Anyone who has studied closely the development of both radio and broadcasting must be struck by the unexpected problems of those who have sought to regulate broadcasting ... To place obstacles in the way of viewers' access to international 'trade' in broadcasting,

in the light of some aim of broadcasting which requires strict national regulation of access to programmes, would simply not work. Governments would find that like King Canute, they could not control the waves.[42]

The pre-1985 Soviet leadership was already beginning to find itself in the position of King Canute. But under Gorbachev, Soviet citizens were given the express right to pick up foreign broadcasts.

The international legal/political framework

During the years of the cold war, the removal of barriers to the flow of ideas across frontiers became a major goal of Western diplomacy. Today that Western goal has been almost totally achieved. Nevertheless, it is likely to raise a number of new issues in the field of international law.

At the present time there is no comprehensive or universally agreed body of international law governing information and the media. Nor is there any universally effective machinery for enforcement. However, freedom of speech and freedom of information have been a focus of international attention for several decades; and they figure prominently in a number of international agreements (all of them actually or potentially relevant to the former USSR). Among these, the following deserve particular mention.

(1) A general right to 'seek, receive, and impart information and ideas' regardless of frontiers has been affirmed, subject to certain qualifications, in two United Nations documents: in Article 20 of the 'Universal Declaration of Human Rights' of 1948,[43] to which the Soviet Union did not adhere; and in Article 19 of the 1966 'International Covenant on Civil and Political Rights'.[44] The Soviet Union, like the United Kingdom, did adhere to this Covenant; but (also like the United Kingdom) it did not sign the optional protocol which allows individuals who claim that their rights have been violated to make direct representations to the UN Human Rights Committee which monitors compliance with the Covenant.

(2) The Helsinki Final Act signed on 1 August 1975[45] also contained provisions which dealt, in particular, with the 'Improvement of the Circulation of, Access to, and Exchange of Information' and with the

'Improvement of Working Conditions for Journalists'. The Final Act did not, of course, have the status of an international treaty.

(3) Conventions adopted by the Council of Europe also guarantee freedom of information across frontiers (in terms broadly similar to those adopted by the UN). The European Conventions are of special importance for two reasons. For one thing, they could in the foreseeable future apply to the former territories of the Soviet Union. In June 1989, the USSR was granted a 'special guest status' at the Council, and it later signed a number of the Council's conventions.[46] In 1990 Eduard Shevardnadze, when he was Soviet Foreign Minister, suggested that the Council's parliamentary assembly might serve as a parliamentary forum for Europe as a whole; and he also said that he believed there were no obstacles to the Soviet Union becoming a full member of the Council.[47]

The second reason why the Council of Europe's conventions could be important is that – unlike the other international agreements mentioned above – they are backed by a judicial mechanism for enforcement. Disputes, including complaints by aggrieved individuals, can under certain conditions be referred to the European Commission on Human Rights and adjudicated upon by the European Court of Human Rights.[48]

It may be added that membership of the Council of Europe already includes three countries of the former Warsaw Pact. Hungary joined the Council in November 1990 and was followed by Czechoslovakia in February 1991 and by Poland in November 1991. If the Council continues to expand its membership eastwards this could have important consequences for the media, because in that case there will be a legal framework, common to both Western and Eastern Europe, for the enforcement of human rights – including media freedom. If Russia were eventually to join the Council of Europe, then the importance of that legal framework would of course be vastly greater.

Freedom of information is not, of course, the only topic with which international media law is concerned. There is a whole range of technical problems (such as the allocations of broadcasting frequencies and the achievement of compatibility between different television systems) which require international coordination.[49] International law in relation to the media clearly suffers from a good many gaps; and the growth of communications across the former Iron Curtain will make it both easier and more urgent to remedy these gaps.

Here the main problems will almost without doubt be political. In the past, the issues of freedom of information, media freedom and the regulation of broadcasting were all treated as being exclusively within the domestic jurisdiction of states. Today these questions are being increasingly internationalized, and the opening up of the former Soviet bloc has accelerated the process.

Joint ventures and foreign ownership

Soviet political reform had, in some ways, totally transformed the opportunities for foreign participation in joint ventures in the USSR. From 1987 onwards, the Soviet authorities began to liberalize the law on foreign investment: already by May 1991 – that is, before the attempted coup – far-reaching legislation had been prepared, which would have allowed foreigners to set up their own wholly owned companies in the Soviet Union.[50] This naturally leads one to ask: what scope does all this offer for foreign investment or participation directed specifically to the media in the former Soviet Union? The question is an important one; but for the time being it is very difficult to make definitive predictions.

Within the former USSR there are many who would wholeheartedly welcome foreign aid or investment in the media. The country's printing and broadcasting equipment is substantially inferior to what is manufactured in the West; and from this point of view alone foreign investment would be enormously beneficial. Furthermore, privatization and the transition to the market have become a high priority for the governments in Moscow and in the republics. Indeed, during Gorbachev's last months in power many in the country saw privatization not just as an economic tool, but as a political lever for breaking the Communist Party's ownership in the fields of publishing and broadcasting.

As of early 1992, however, the role of joint ventures in general was somewhat limited, despite impressive appearances to the contrary. During 1989 the overall number of such ventures rose by a factor of 6.7 and, as of 1 January 1990, the total number of joint ventures was reported to have risen to 1,274 (of which 947, that is, almost three-quarters, were based in the Russian republic).[51] During 1990 and after, the number soared still further: by the end of March 1991, it had risen almost threefold, to 3,200. In 1991 it was estimated, however, that joint ventures as a whole contributed no more than 0.5 per cent to the Soviet gross national product.[52] It is possible that this figure understates their importance, since many joint ventures exist on paper but have not yet become operational. However, the picture so far is of a growing number of small-scale undertakings whose total impact on the economy is not very great.

What has just been said relates to joint ventures of all kinds. So far as the media are concerned, developments have been significant but are still limited. We noted in the last chapter that the 1992 media law (Article 7) debars foreigners from acting as the founders of Russian newspapers. Nevertheless, joint media ventures have been set up. Under an agreement signed in October 1991, programmes of the BBC Russian Service are to be regularly rebroadcast on a weekly basis in Moscow by Radio Rossiya, which will in turn regularly send members of its staff to gain work experience with the BBC Russian Service.[53] The German broadcasting organization Deutsche Welle has arranged for the transmission of its programmes by certain local Russian stations.[54] National stations in the republics appear to have attracted help from abroad – although the situation is fluid and information is often obtainable only by word of mouth. In July 1991 a Russian-language edition of the American-owned *Reader's Digest* began to appear in Moscow.[55] In early 1992, the *New York Times* announced that it would be regularly publishing selected Russian translations of its articles. These would be distributed in Russia by *Moscow News*, and the *New York Times* would receive a share of the advertising revenue.[56] As far as Britain is concerned, however, its role in joint media undertakings has until now (except for the BBC agreement) been barely noticeable.

All this makes something of a contrast to Eastern Europe – and to Hungary in particular – where Western investors in the media have been very active since 1989. Indeed in Hungary virtually every daily newspaper is now partly foreign-owned.[57] Nevertheless, East European experience may well offer lessons for the former USSR. Eastern Europe's newspapers badly need foreign capital and can be bought up comparatively cheaply. But that does not make them profitable, because they usually require huge investments for the modernization of plant and training of staff; and in Hungary (as in the former USSR) the distribution system for newspapers is notoriously inefficient. Advertising is not an adequate source of revenue. (As a British correspondent asked: 'How soon will there be consumers prosperous enough to advertise to?'[58]) There seems to be no guarantee of a profit for foreign investors, even in the medium term. In any case not all of the problems have been to do solely with economics. Market principles have sometimes pushed the press in a down-market direction: they have not always been helpful to quality journalism. And there has been a certain backlash against the wave of newspaper acquisitions by Westerners. In Hungary in 1990, a parliamentary commission was set up to investigate the problem.[59] Concern about the pattern of foreign ownership of the media has been apparent also in other countries of Eastern Europe.[60]

In the former USSR, the media are generally in a worse state, economically, than they are in Eastern Europe. The political turmoil, as well as the recent 'war of laws' between the centre and the republics, will also have been a deterrent to foreign investors and probably explains why they have been slow off the mark. That is not to say that the former USSR offers no commercial attractions at all. In some cases it may do so: for example, for foreigners who want to 'get their foot in the door' in the expectation of better times ahead, or for those whose knowledge of the ropes in the former Soviet Union could give them an advantage over potential foreign rivals. It is naturally possible that Western newspaper proprietors are planning to invest in the near future, but there was no clear sign of this as of early 1992. If foreign investment were to be commercially advantageous in the normal sense, at least two major conditions would have to be satisfied. First, local law would have to allow for the unrestricted repatriation of profits in hard currency. Second, there would have to be greater all-round stability as well as a clearer legal framework, so that investors know what their rights are. None of this is to deny that foreigners might have political or non-financial motives for lending assistance to the local media. This seems to be much of the reason behind the help from abroad which is being given at present.

To sum up: the growth of Soviet openness in relation to the outside world after 1987 was colossal, and virtually all the goals which the West set out to achieve at Helsinki in 1975 have been realized. Political change in Russia – coupled with the progress of communications technology, which was occurring anyway – may well, in the foreseeable future, open an entirely new chapter in international contacts and communications.

These will highlight a number of other problems – such as the economic barriers to migration and the problems of regulating transfrontier television – which will move higher up the political agenda, now that the old Iron Curtain has disappeared.

First, however, one has to look at the strains on the new openness caused by the country's current crisis. For if openness or free expression runs into trouble, this would naturally hinder progress towards a more open international community.

5

DOMESTIC POLITICAL EFFECTS: A BACKLASH ON MEDIA POLICY?

By the middle of 1991, the reality of Soviet openness had become undeniable. Its benefits were already obvious. But its side-effects were often disturbing. The advent of free information and free speech after more than 70 years seems to have acted as a trigger – which undermined not only dictatorship but authority in general. It produced revelations about the Soviet past which came as a severe shock to many Russians; and it played a major part in the rise of nationalism (including ethnic conflict) among the country's non-Russian peoples. All in all, openness accelerated, even if it did not cause, the general crisis of morale and legitimacy. This led to talk of collapse or disintegration; and by mid-1991 it had prompted practically all the reforming leaders of 1985 to desert Gorbachev. Even more seriously, it raised the prospect of a return to authoritarian rule – a prospect which continued to be discussed even after the failure of the August coup.

It cannot be taken for granted that the danger of an authoritarian backlash is finally past. And, needless to say, if dictatorship were to return, or if openness were, for whatever reason, to 'turn sour', then this would radically affect any assessment of the consequences of the new openness for international relations. How far, then, is this pessimistic scenario justified? And if authoritarianism did return, how serious is the danger of a return to

45

the totalitarian *status quo ante*? These are the questions to which this chapter is addressed. But it is difficult to discuss them without examining glasnost in the context of Soviet society as a whole.

No one imagines that glasnost was the only reason for the country's current turmoil. As a rule it is not openness but economic crisis which leads to destabilization. The contrast between post-Franco Spain and post-Tito Yugoslavia seems to bear this out. Where Gorbachev was concerned, the economy was, almost from the start, his Achilles heel. Much of the original trouble stemmed not from glasnost but from economic misjudgments (notably a failure to monitor the budget deficit).[1] In the event, Gorbachev embarked on democratization at almost exactly the moment when (partly because of the fall in living standards) his own popularity among the voters was declining.

The sequel was the unleashing of forces which were not only pluralistic but centrifugal. 1990 saw a rash of declarations of sovereignty or independence by the newly elected parliaments of the republics – who insisted that their own laws took precedence over those of the USSR. This in turn led to the 'war of laws' between the centre and the republics and, most seriously of all, to the confrontation in 1990-91 between Gorbachev and Yeltsin. The ensuing legislative paralysis inevitably aggravated the economic paralysis as well.

Glasnost and the crisis of authority

By 1990 and 1991, members of the Soviet public were openly complaining that the shortages were worse than they had been under Brezhnev. The extent of disillusionment with reform was highlighted by a survey carried out in the Russian republic in July 1991 which asked people whether, if they had known in 1985 where the reforms would lead, they would have supported them. To this question the replies were: Yes, 23 per cent; No, 52 per cent. The failing economy was not the only reason for popular dissatisfaction, but it was clearly one of the main reasons. A further poll conducted in the following month asked the question: 'Which of society's problems do you find most menacing?' At the head of the list were rising prices (mentioned by 69 per cent of respondents) and the shortage of foodstuffs and goods (named by 56 per cent). Third on the list was the rise in crime (mentioned by 28 per cent).[2]

It is against this background of falling living standards and declining public morale that one has to consider the impact of glasnost. From 1987 onwards the limits of permissible criticism were extended almost without interruption – so as to allow not just criticism within the system but criticism of the system itself. More honest reporting from abroad soon led to an open admission of the huge prosperity gap between the Soviet Union and the West. This, far from being played down in the Soviet media, was now emphasized in the most public way possible. Already in 1989, an article in *Argumenty i fakty*, one of the most widely read Soviet weekly newspapers, which at that time had a print-run of over 22 million copies, informed its readers that 'our living standards are at best on a level with such ... countries as Ireland, Argentina, Portugal and Brazil, but in many respects we have substantially lagged behind even them,' and that 'in our grain harvests we lag behind Turkey, Pakistan, Bangladesh and Nicaragua'.[3] Scviet statistical publications began to include international comparisons showing the USSR in an unfavourable light.[4]

At the same time, openness about Soviet history steadily grew, at least from 1988 onwards. In May of that year Soviet television put on a newsreel film of one of Stalin's show trials of the 1930s.[5] In the summer of 1988 it was announced that all history examinations in schools were to be cancelled pending the preparation of an entirely new school history book.[6] In 1990 that history book appeared (it was described as 'a temporary transitional textbook') in an edition of 2,905,000 copies. It contained information not only about the GULAG and the failings of Soviet leaders from Stalin onwards: it even included excerpts from a letter sent to the Soviet leadership by Andrei Sakharov in the early 1970s. For Soviet schoolchildren this was something entirely novel. It was yet another sign that the repudiation of a large part of the Soviet past had become official policy.[7]

The most immediate impact of the new glasnost was on the non-Russian nationalities. It led, in early 1988, to the open voicing of Armenia's claim for the return of Nagorny Karabakh (the Armenian-inhabited enclave inside Azerbaijan which had been assigned to that republic in 1923); and the revival of this claim led to violent clashes between Armenians and Azerbaijanis. Meanwhile, among the peoples of the Baltic, glasnost had an even more powerful effect – because it unleashed a public discussion of the 1939 Molotov-Ribbentrop pact and its secret protocol, which had assigned the Baltic states to the Soviet sphere of influence. The existence of this secret protocol was finally confirmed by Alexander Yakovlev on behalf of the Soviet leadership on 18 August 1989, just five days before the pact's 50th anniversary.[8] It produced an immediate sequel. On the actual anniversary of the pact, Baltic nationalists formed a 'human chain' stretching without interruption from Estonia in the north to Lithuania in the south in order to affirm their insistence that the Soviet annexation of their countries had been illegal.

No less far-reaching in the longer run was the impact of openness on ordinary Russians. At least one Soviet writer, in the summer of 1989, saw the wave of revelations as a source of possible disillusionment, and even as a potential threat to democracy:

> The expectation of rapid results and the lack of such results produced a feeling of dissatisfaction and irritation, a passionate desire for perceptible changes and concrete results of some kind, a feeling of impatience. Besides that, a great many people were reduced to a state of psychological malaise. The destruction of old myths deprived their lives of a sense of cohesion. They got nothing to replace the sense of cohesion which they had lost; and having failed to find any substitute on their own, they remained inwardly at odds with themselves. As a result they developed roughly the following picture of their lives: the past is disgraceful, the present is monstrous and the future is uncertain and unpredictable. In this psychological state, the masses are prepared to accept any leader who says: 'I know what has to be done and how to do it.'[9]

A year later, Academician Tatyana Zaslavskaya, the well-known Soviet sociologist and head of the recently founded Centre for the Study of Public Opinion in Moscow, spoke in a similar vein of a dangerous moral vacuum in the wake of disillusionment:

> Disappointment in socialism is one reason for the crumbling moral foundations. Eternal moral values such as honour, duty, morality and patriotism had been tied to socialist ideology. Now this ideology is falling apart, people are being left without moral guidelines. They no longer know what is good and what is bad.[10]

Opinion surveys – apart from showing a steady decline in the popularity of Mikhail Gorbachev and of the Communist Party – also revealed deep divisions of attitude towards Soviet history. According to one such survey carried out in Moscow in the summer of 1990, 21.9 per cent of respondents agreed with the statement that 'All our society's misfortunes began with the October revolution: there must be a return to the system which existed up to October 1917', whilst a slightly smaller proportion – 21.1 per cent – agreed that 'It is necessary to complete perestroika within the framework of the socialist choice'. A slightly larger group – 28.2 per cent – supported the view that 'What is important is a moral renewal of man and society and this cannot be realized without a revival of religion and the enhancement of the role of the church'. The two most common responses – by over 48 per cent of those interviewed – were that 'The past cannot be altered: it is necessary to work better and then life will be better, but discussions about socialism and capitalism have no particular sense'; and that 'the main thing … is a revival of … national culture'. Consequently, as one sociologist then pointed out, 'the socialist choice is not at the present time a basis for consolidation'.[11]

It is not hard to see why the Gorbachev reforms were so much more admired abroad than they were at home. For millions of Soviet citizens, glasnost meant little more than an unprecedented freedom to complain about an almost unprecedented drop in living standards and a particularly tyrannical history. All this helps to explain the mood of pessimism, and indeed negativism, among the Soviet public during the Gorbachev years. Glasnost merely led, quite inevitably, to the voicing of grievances which could not quickly be remedied.

Making an inventory of the damage done by the Soviet regime in the past is of course an unavoidable and long-drawn-out business. That is not to say that all the findings should be accepted uncritically at face value. Forecasts of imminent disaster became commonplace and were sometimes proved wrong. There was the occasion in New York in September 1989 when Boris Yeltsin was asked how much time Mikhail Gorbachev had to show progress, and replied: 'Not more than one year and probably about six months, I would say.'[12] Shortly after that, during a visit to Tokyo, he was reported as saying: 'The Soviet Union is faced with a crisis and could destroy itself within as little as three months.'[13] In December 1990, an even more apocalyptic vision was presented by the leading economist, Academician Stanislav Shatalin – who told an American interviewer that 'our malady is so serious … that the time remaining to us can be counted not in months but in days'.[14]

It would no doubt be unwise to assume that every piece of negative material in the present-day Russian press can be accepted without scrutiny. But the very abundance of this negative material is itself a result of the prevailing mood in Russia, where such material is certain to find a receptive audience.

To sum up, glasnost was clearly not the main cause of the country's crisis, but it was a major contributory cause. It helped to make society more pluralistic – and also more centrifugal. By undermining public morale, it indirectly undermined the confidence without which it is impossible for any economic system to function. Nor was it always a healing force. In many cases, it merely focused attention on deep-seated ailments which could not, in the short run, be cured. All this helps to explain the disorientation, the pessimism and the anger which it only too often engendered.

Authoritarianism, communist and anti-communist

It is therefore only natural to ask: if the crisis does continue, can Russia's embryonic openness or freedom of speech in the long run survive? Is there a danger of that freedom of expression becoming, so to speak, a 'self-limiting' phenomenon – something which tends by its nature to aggravate the crisis of authority and so increase the likelihood of an authoritarian backlash? Is there a danger that the frequent predictions of disaster in the now uncensored media could become self-fulfilling prophecies? The problem here goes deeper than that of power struggles between leaders or even the danger of further coups; the real issue is what follows if or when the old order is finally swept away. The 'post-communist' era has placed a number of new topics on the agenda: privatization of the economy (to which we shall return in a moment); nationalism, populism, 'anti-communist radicalism' and, of course, the break-up of the former USSR. All these things are very understandable. The question is whether any of them automatically lead to democracy or freedom of speech. Even if the bulk of the new political forces are indeed pledged to a democratic path, they could still face grave difficulties, when confronted with a crisis in a country whose democratic and legal traditions are extremely weak.

The dangers to democracy (and therefore to freedom of speech) come partly from certain political movements, partly from the future attitude of the military and partly from impersonal factors, such as economic crisis. The open discussion of these issues in the Russian press has made it easier than before to identify the dangers. They can be considered under several headings.

There is, in the first place, the threat from conservative communists. It would be premature to write them off completely. Even after the failure of the coup, speculation continued about a possible second coup.[15] What unites the hardline communists is their readiness to use force if necessary to try to halt the further disintegration of Russia. Their hostility to freedom of speech can be seen from the rigid censorship which they imposed during the two days when the August coup was in progress.

A related threat to democracy and free speech comes from the forces of authoritarian Russian nationalism. Its hallmarks are a strong chauvinism, a frequent overtone of anti-semitism and (on the face of it) an anti-communism. Nationalists of this variety will often blame Russia's misfortunes on the legacy of Bolshevism (or sometimes on alleged Jewish influence).[16] But they agree with the communist hardliners in advocating a more disciplined society and in wanting to halt the break-up of the former USSR. In the Russian presidential elections of 1991, one of the candidates, Vladimir Zhirinovsky, argued that 'today the Russians are the most humiliated nation in the country', and he campaigned on an avowedly nationalistic platform, which included the preservation of the USSR within its then borders.[17] Zhirinovsky did better at the polls than expected: he finished in third place, with 7.9 per cent of the vote.[18] However, he and others like him discredited themselves in August 1991 by supporting the coup. (As as a result the 'Liberal Democratic Party', which he led, was suspended.) A prominent Russian public opinion expert observed shortly afterwards that 'conservative Russian nationalism wields no appreciable influence on society'.[19] This may be true in the short run: it is less certain in the longer run, if the economy continues to get worse.

Yet another threat to democracy and free speech comes, in certain cases, from anti-communist *non*-Russian nationalism. The best known example is, of course, the record of former President Zviad Gamsakhurdia in what was once Soviet Georgia. In May 1991 Gamsakhurdia, who had already won power in a general election, was overwhelmingly elected by popular vote to the newly created post of president. However, of the five other candidates who ran against him, none was allowed to publish his programme in the republican press.[20] The ensuing civil war and the overthrow of Gamsakhurdia in early 1992 made worldwide headline news. Clearly there was less press freedom here than in Gorbachev's Russia.

So much, then, for some of the forces which are openly hostile to glasnost and free speech. As to the radicals led by Boris Yeltsin, they have been in power for only a short time: therefore it is rather early to judge them. They have certainly been associated with some important pluses. The press became, perhaps, freer to comment than ever before. (I have heard this even from among the staff of *Pravda*; and the content of Russian newspapers seems to bear this out.) The other side of the coin is that Yeltsin and his colleagues have sometimes appeared to bypass the law in ways which could potentially undermine civil liberties, including perhaps the freedom of the press. One case in point was Yeltsin's decree of 6 November 1991 permanently dissolving the Soviet Communist Party. Politically, this may have been unimportant, since the party had already collapsed. It appears nevertheless that, under existing Russian laws, only a court has the power to dissolve a political party against its will; and Yeltsin's decree did not even mention the courts. An attempt was later made to challenge the ban in Russia's newly established Constitutional Court, though the outcome of the appeal is, at the time of writing, unknown.[21] But the ban itself had obvious legal dangers. The tradition of governments which disregarded their own laws has been notorious throughout Soviet history; and if the tradition were to continue, it would be a bad augury. It is, after all, only a short step from banning a political party to banning a newspaper.[22]

In the meantime, the Chairman of the new Constitutional Court, Professor Valery Zorkin, went on record as accusing the country's new leaders of 'legal nihilism'.[23] Other warnings about threats to media freedom have been quite commonly made in the Russian press in the months since the failed coup.[24] The potential threat of the government exerting economic pressure on newspapers has already been mentioned in Chapter 3. All in all, therefore, it is a little early to say with confidence that the end of Soviet communism necessarily spells media freedom.

Even more disturbing, if true, were reports early in 1992 of possible plans by the authorities to put Gorbachev, Shevardnadze and Alexander Yakovlev on trial on charges of misusing Communist Party funds (apparently on the grounds that they failed to prevent the funding of foreign communist parties). There is, however, the gravest doubt that any such trial would be fair; and it is somewhat surprising that the Western media were so slow to pick up the story.[25]

But the health of the country's embryonic democracy cannot be assessed only by reference to the politicians. Just as important, perhaps, where political and media freedom are concerned, is the prevailing public mood – which in Russia today is not invariably conducive to toleration. A Russian psychologist writing in 1991 identified two prevalent moods: first, anger and aggressiveness; second, weariness and apathy. Poll findings have corroborated this analysis.[26] The aggressive atmosphere has now, so it seems, had an intimidating effect on the work of the courts. By 1990, according to one lawyer, judges were subject to rather less interference from the communist authorities, but were sometimes under pressure from what amounted to mob rule.[27]

It appears, then, that the threshold of toleration in the country is sometimes low. And, apart from all this, the country's traditions have done little to foster a climate of dialogue between political opponents. The Moscow weekly *Literaturnaya gazeta*, which is now politically independent, has several times called attention to this problem. An article in early 1991 highlighted the way in which the language of confrontation had taken root. Conservative rhetoric, it suggested, could be identified by such key words as 'disorders', 'vandalism', 'permissiveness', 'demagogues', 'destructive forces', 'so-called' and 'allegedly'; whereas the rhetoric of the radicals was marked by such expressions as 'KGB agents', 'Bolshevist tyranny', 'ideological stupefaction', 'imperial thinking', 'red fascists', 'party mafia', 'party bosses' and 'partocracy'.[28]

In the early summer of 1991, another feature in the same paper discussed the phenomenon which Russians now refer to as 'neo-Bolshevism' – that is, an intolerance towards those who think differently, and sometimes a readiness to fight communism by its own methods. It quoted current statements to illustrate what it meant – ranging from claims that 'pseudo-perestroika' would result in 'disintegration, collapse and impoverishment' to charges that 'The CPSU [Soviet Communist Party] is a criminal organization against which action should be taken'. 'Today it is already apparent', the paper said, 'that neo-Bolshevism has identically affected people on the left, the right and the centre.' And a Soviet historian, after recalling the sequence of events during the 1917 revolution, added a warning to some of the anti-communist radicals: 'You have taken from the Bolsheviks the worst which they had to offer. You should not make the mistakes which Lenin made in 1917.'[29]

Finally, when discussing the prospects for democracy in the former USSR, the obvious question arises: where do privatization and the transition to the market fit in? The general issue of the market economy does not concern us here. The immediate question is whether economic reform and political democracy are compatible. If they are not, then freedom of the media could be seriously at risk. It is sometimes taken for granted that once a democratically elected government has come to power, the public will regard it as 'legitimate' and will therefore be more willing to accept sacrifices. Although this may in certain cases be true, the reverse proposition can also be argued. A government which depends on its voters is sometimes more reluctant to impose harsh austerity, no matter what the economic experts advise. This is particularly true of the former USSR, where those living below the poverty line represent a large part of the electorate.[30] But if democratic government is unable to halt economic collapse, the danger of dictatorship is all too real. The question is not whether the former Soviet Union can move over to the market, but whether it can do so without destroying democracy and free speech in the process.

All this leads to another scenario, which in the months prior to the failed coup had caused some discussion in the Soviet press – the possibility of military rule, not in order to prevent economic reform but in order to achieve it. One writer in 1990 sketched out this scenario in an article entitled 'To the market, under cover of the army?' An essential precondition for a market economy was, he said, a stability of laws and economic ties. He went on to note that 'when a transition is made from a socialized (or a devastated or just a bad) economy to an efficient market economy, this is quite often achieved under a state of emergency or martial law', as in the cases of Greece (under the Colonels), South Korea or Chile. The author of the article was not advocating such a course, but he ended by asking a very pertinent question: 'How are we to travel along the knife-edge of democratization without falling either into military dictatorship or into the chaos of disintegration? We shall have to think about this, no matter how disagreeable such reflections may be.'[31] The failed coup of 1991 provided an interim answer to this question; but it may be some years before the danger of a return to dictatorship can be finally ruled out.

A return to the status quo ante?

Assuming for a moment a worst-case scenario, with democracy collapsing amidst anarchy and economic breakdown, would this mean a return to the earlier 'totalitarian' stereotype, with glasnost totally reversed, as in Czechoslovakia after the Soviet invasion of 1968? There are several reasons for discounting this likelihood.

If Russian democracy breaks down, the resulting scenario would be closer to Latin America than to Brezhnev. (Indeed Russians sometimes use the term 'Pinochetization', a term which has become familiar to Western Sovietologists, in order to underline the Chilean parallel.) This would mean a transition to the market based on coercion, possibly aided by foreign capital and underpinned by a populist or military-backed regime without any clear ideology – but still with nuclear weapons. Following the break-up of the USSR, the emergence of dictatorships in some of the republics would be very possible. Such a regime (or regimes) would probably not emerge under communist auspices and could emerge simply under the impact of crisis. Curbs on the media would be likely. But they would be substantially different from those used by the Soviet authorities in the past.

The initial weapons against the media might well be economic – cutting off the paper supply to recalcitrant newspapers, hampering their circulation or perhaps imposing fines. The experience of dictatorships with a market economy clearly shows that private ownership of the media is not in itself a safeguard for freedom of expression. Government harassment, or the threat of financial ruin for newspapers which persistently fall foul of the authorities, can be very effective in silencing criticism. Press restrictions, such as those which existed in South Africa during the 1980s and before, can also be effective in keeping the public ignorant of what is happening in its own country. And any future dictatorship might, of course, reimpose some of the old restrictions on foreign journalists as well as cutting back on freedom of information.

Anything like this would, needless to say, be a severe blow to democracy – particularly since dictatorships once installed can be hard to get rid of. Nevertheless, it would not amount to 'totalitarianism' as the term has traditionally been used. There is a great difference between the restrictions, for example in Chile under Pinochet, which silenced criticism, and the old pre-1985 Soviet propaganda system, which maintained the fiction of a 'unanimous' public opinion and imposed a positive duty on journalists to praise government policies. No future regime in the former USSR would have very much rational incentive to go back to that earlier system – because it would lack all credibility with its own public.

It is now almost certainly too late to undo the consequences of glasnost, because the political skeletons are out of the cupboard (mentioned even in school history books) and naturally cannot be put back. Even a severe curtailment of press freedom (falling short of totalitarianism) would be counterproductive because it would simply increase the audience for Western broadcasts. As for curtailment of contacts with the outside world, this could involve a loss of international goodwill, which the successor states to the USSR would think twice about incurring.

In short, then, a continuing social crisis could well lead to the curtailment of media freedom; but certain achievements of glasnost have become irreversible. It is possible that glasnost could 'turn sour' in the sense of producing disillusionment both in the former USSR and in the outside world. It is also conceivable that, as a result of a series of internal conflicts within the former USSR, confrontation could turn into fragmentation, thus eroding initial optimism about a New World Order. But, whatever the uncertainties may be, the restoration of the traditional closed society seems less and less likely. Soviet openness does seem to have set in motion a series of international changes which it is already too late to reverse.

6

RUSSIAN OPENNESS AND THE OUTSIDE WORLD

Russian openness: a two-way process?
The preceding chapters have concentrated on the nature and effects of openness within the USSR. They have suggested that, although freedom of speech and information may have caused grave problems, nevertheless a return to the old-style closed society is unlikely in the extreme: Russian openness, in some form, is here to stay. This brings us directly to the question of the implications of openness for international relations. Granted that openness was a key factor in breaking the mould of Soviet. politics, might it also have, or have had, an impact on the outside world? To put it in a slightly different way: has Soviet or Russian openness been a mainly one-way process, providing opportunities for the West to influence events in the former USSR? Or could it be a process which operates in both directions? In the rest of this chapter these two questions will be discussed in turn.

Glasnost and the impact of the West on the Soviet Union
The impact of Western ideas on the (former) USSR was of course obvious, but is no less important for that reason. In a number of ways it began long before 1985. Subsequently, when the Soviet authorities

gradually pulled down the information barriers, Western influence in the country rapidly grew. Two major examples of this were, first, the management of the economy, where Western advice was, and is, increasingly being sought; and, second, the role of foreign broadcasts during the 1991 failed coup, of which more later. In addition, there are a host of minor examples of Western influence which are now becoming too numerous even to monitor. In 1990, for instance, it was reported that Russian radical politicians from Moscow were seeking advice from politicians in Washington on the art of political coalition-building.[1] The public in Russia and other areas of the USSR became far more exposed to the West than at any previous time in their history. In June 1991, American films were said to account for 31 out of the 64 films showing in Moscow.[2] For millions of ordinary Russians, the West clearly held a fascination. It may not be irrelevant to mention the results of a Russian poll of 1991 which had asked: 'Who, in your view, is the most popular woman in the world?' Some 55 per cent named Margaret Thatcher.[3]

The list of similar examples could be greatly extended. The crux of the matter was that Western ideas were bound to have an impact on the USSR because they catered for an enormous demand. In what follows our approach must necessarily be selective and will focus on two areas, namely the availability of Western books and the role of Western broadcasting in the USSR, both before and after 1985. First of all, however, something must be said about the effect of Soviet 'new thinking' in opening up the country to ideas from the outside world.

The abandonment of the 'enemy image' of the West

Western ideas did not gain a hold in the Soviet Union all at once. They grew partly because of the West's unaided efforts (mainly in the field of broadcasting) and – to a dramatic extent – as a result of Moscow's 'new thinking' in the late 1980s. The pre-1985 Soviet leadership had indeed advocated detente, as well as the development of (controlled) contacts with the outside world. But earlier generations of Soviet leaders had all been committed to a doctrine of fundamental East-West antagonism (falling short of war) which they presented in terms of an 'ideological struggle'. This basically negative view of the West was reflected in the whole official terminology: in the use of such familiar words as 'bourgeois' and 'imperialist'. It shaped the entire manner in which Western society was presented by the then Soviet propaganda machine. The West was constantly portrayed as as an adversary in a state of irreversible long-term decline – and perhaps all the more menacing for that very reason. Indeed, on 7 November 1982, only three days before Brezhnev's death, a *Pravda* article had described capitalism as something which was 'inwardly rotting' but was nevertheless 'a powerful and dangerous enemy'.[4]

In the later 1980s, as a result of Soviet 'new thinking', this 'enemy image' of the West was by degrees totally repudiated. One of the first signs of change came as early as January 1986, when an *Izvestiya* commentator called for changes in the reporting of foreign countries by the Soviet media; and just over a year later a letter to *Pravda* had urged it to drop 'slogan-mongering' in its coverage of the West.[5] In November 1987, a Soviet deputy Foreign Minister, Vladimir Petrovsky, denounced what he described as 'the vicious practice of spreading disinformation about the domestic and foreign policies of other states'.[6] (The context indicated that he was including his own country in the criticism.) In July 1988, Eduard Shevardnadze, in the course of a long speech at the Soviet Ministry of Foreign Affairs, explicitly stated that 'the "enemy image" in all its dimensions is a hindrance to the restructuring of international relations on a moral and civilized foundation'.[7]

The abandonment of the 'enemy image' was to have dramatic consequences within the Soviet Union; and it did so at two levels. First, the senior Soviet establishment probably became better informed about the outside world, because Soviet diplomats began to send more candid reports from abroad. In earlier years they had not always done so, preferring, as one eye-witness said, 'to make the information which they sent to Moscow "correspond" with the views which already prevailed there'.[8] Shevardnadze seemed to confirm this when, in the remarks quoted above, he said that diplomatic reporting had changed for the better and that 'in most cases, it has become more objective, I would say more honest'.[9] The effect of more candid information on the reshaping of Soviet foreign policy must itself have been considerable.

Secondly, and even more obviously, the abandonment of the 'enemy image' of the West had a profound effect on members of the Soviet public at large. They were in effect officially told that their own leaders had been giving them a false or gravely distorted picture of the outside world for more than 70 years. By 1990 the Soviet media, instead of

Table 6.1   Books translated in the USSR from English into Russian for selected years, 1981–9

	1981	1984	1985	1986	1987	1988	1989
Number of titles	614	595	563	602	568	586	640
Number of copies printed (millions)	50.2	68.2	44.9	67.9	66.8	59.8	91.8

Source: *Pechat' v SSSR* (Moscow: Finansy i statistika) for the relevant years. Figures are excerpted from Table 11 (for 1981, 1984 and 1985) and from Table 6 (for 1986-9).

portraying the West as an 'imperialist' adversary in a state of terminal crisis, had begun to refer to the West as an integral part of the 'world civilization' to which Russia must now seek to return.[10] In this entirely new climate, Soviet citizens became exposed on a massive scale to Western ideas – through their own domestic media. (In the past many of these ideas had been known only to a small band of dissidents.) The official repudiation of communism by those who came to power in Moscow after the August coup can only have accelerated this whole process.

The influx of Western books
The exposure of the Russian public to the Western media has now reached a stage where it can no longer be measured statistically. Figures do, however, exist – both for the early and for the late 1980s – as to the number of English books translated annually into Russian and published in the Soviet Union. Table 6.1 gives some idea of the trend during the 1980s.

The translation of books from English occurred on a large scale even before 1985, despite fluctuations. What is particularly noteworthy is the sharp upward trend in 1989, the last year for which overall figures are available; and there are grounds for believing that by 1991 the number of books translated from English was rising even more steeply. This can be inferred from current book lists published in Moscow, which indicate that in June 1991 66 English books were published or reissued, and that by August the figure had risen to 147.[11]

There are, unfortunately, no figures to show exactly what *kinds* of Western books were being translated in past years. But there can be no doubt that the situation today is radically different from what it once was.

Publication now depends on commercial, not ideological considerations; and this has stimulated a demand for precisely the kind of literature which the old regime would have disapproved of. A very few examples should be enough to demonstrate this. Thus, 1988 saw the publication of Arthur Koestler's *Darkness at Noon*; George Orwell's *1984* was published in the following year; as also was a chapter of Robert Conquest's *Harvest of Sorrow*, which describes the Ukrainian famine following collectivization in the 1930s. Books either published or planned for publication in 1990 and 1991 included Professor Friedrich Hayek's *The Road to Serfdom*, Winston Churchill's *The Second World War*, the selected speeches of Ronald Reagan, articles and speeches by Pope Paul II, and Milovan Djilas on *The Face of Totalitarianism*.

These examples all refer to books published or planned for publication prior to the August coup. The volume of Western books is likely to increase still further in the future. Moreover, these books have not been confined to politics. Works of fiction, such as Agatha Christie or Frederick Forsyth, are also making their presence felt. And, last but not least, recent months have seen an entirely new body of translated literature on the themes of entrepreneurship and the market. Planned translations from English include such titles as *How to Become Enterprising and Rich – with American Methods*, *Self-confidence: The Road to Business Success*, *How to Settle the Problems of Marketing*, *First Principles of Economics* and a *Commmercial Dictionary*, as well as much else of a similar kind.[12] The demand for Western economic know-how is likely to produce a continuing demand for Western books of this type.

Western broadcasting to Russia: the August coup

For the Western media, the August 1991 coup was something of a historical landmark, because they were not merely reporters of events, but participants: they were a crucial factor in the coup's defeat. During those two days, the Soviet audience for Western broadcasts evidently ran into many millions – as indicated by the figures in Table 6.2, which are based on interviews carried out in a number of areas of the USSR shortly afterwards. Radio Liberty, an American-sponsored station based on Munich, broadcasts 24 hours a day in Russian and a number of other languages of the former USSR, and has always sought to operate as an alternative domestic radio. This may help to explain why it won the

Table 6.2   Percentage of respondents who listened in Russian to Radio Liberty, the Voice of America and the BBC during the attempted coup (19–21 August 1991)

	Moscow	Akademgorodok	Novosibirsk	Lithuania
RL	30	26	14	35
VOA	15	18	11	18
BBC	18	15	6	18

Source: Interviews carried out on behalf of Radio Liberty. I am grateful to Eugene Parta, the head of audience research at Radio Liberty, for providing these data.

largest audience. It will be seen that the BBC and Voice of America were, very generally speaking, on a level with each other. In a small but significant way, foreign television also made its presence felt. People in Moscow or other cities who had satellite dish aerials were able to watch CNN, which provided live coverage of a press conference given by Boris Yeltsin on 19 August, and also showed pictures of the anti-putsch demonstrations outside the White House, the Russian parliament. A British journalist saw the staff in a Moscow hotel watching these CNN reports – of events in their own city – which were not available from domestic television.[13] In the history of revolutions and putsches, this must have been something entirely without precedent.

Throughout the crisis the Western media provided a sometimes instantaneous two-way channel of communication between the outside world and those resisting the putsch. The results were clearly to be seen. The local censorship was rendered ineffectual. Western governments were able to follow events almost minute by minute and to convey their support to Yeltsin and Gorbachev. Gorbachev himself, when forcibly detained in the Crimea, was wholly dependent on Western broadcasts for reliable information. They were vitally important in enabling him to stand firm against his captors and resist their attempts to make him sign away his powers. On his return to Moscow after being set free, he singled out the BBC for special mention and described how he had managed to tune into a report from a BBC correspondent who was actually in the besieged Russian parliament. He also went out of his way 'to thank both Soviet and foreign journalists' for what they had done.[14] It would be difficult to imagine a clearer acknowledgment of the Western media's role.

Western broadcasts to the USSR: their long-term role

The impact of Western broadcasts on the Soviet public predated glasnost by several decades. The BBC began to broadcast in Russian in March 1946, and the Voice of America began to do so in February of the following year. Radio Liberty (originally run under the auspices of the CIA and known as 'Radio Liberation') started its broadcasts to the USSR in March 1953.

It was impossible in the earlier years to measure the size of the audience for these broadcasts – although the Soviet authorities did carry out their own private investigations. (In 1968, an officially sponsored but unpublished survey of the readership of *Pravda* found that some 6 to 8 per cent of those interviewed admitted to getting information from foreign broadcasts.[15]) Meanwhile from the 1970s onwards, Radio Liberty began to conduct its own systematic audience research, usually based on interviews with short-term Soviet visitors to the West. Its own calculations (which involved the use of a computer simulation model aimed at getting a representative picture) suggested a very substantial audience indeed. In 1984, the last year before Gorbachev came to power, it estimated that Voice of America broadcasts beamed to the USSR were heard at least once a week by 14-18 per cent of the Soviet adult population aged 16 and over. The corresponding figure for Radio Liberty was 8-12 per cent; and for the BBC Russian Service 7-10 per cent. At this time, of course, all the three stations were still being jammed. Even so, a sizeable segment of Soviet society was motivated to listen; and it was all the more important for being disproportionately concentrated among the more educated groups.[16] It may be added that, in the late 1970s, Radio Liberty estimated the Soviet audience for all broadcasts from the West during the course of a year as amounting to 67.3 million adults over the age of 16. This would have been equivalent to 37 per cent of the adult population at the time.[17]

Clearly, then, Western broadcasts had won a vast Soviet audience long before the era of glasnost. That audience still exists, although political change in the former USSR has faced Western stations with an entirely new type of challenge. The ending of censorship has made the Russian media far more interesting and attractive to their own listeners, who now have less incentive to tune into foreign stations. On the other hand, it is now far easier for these stations to find out what their listeners' interests are. Their listening habits seem to be changing – although still in a state of some flux.

In this new situation, the main Western beneficiary – in terms of the size of its audience – appears to have been Radio Liberty (which in August 1991, after the failed coup, was authorized for the first time to open an office in Moscow). Its own research indicated that between 1987 (when it was still jammed) and the second half of 1989 (after all jamming had stopped) its average weekly audience nearly doubled – from 9.6 per cent of the adult population to 16.8 per cent. Over the same period, the weekly audience for the Voice of America slightly fell – from 13.8 per cent to 13 per cent; and that of the BBC Russian Service also dropped – from 8.9 per cent to 6.4 per cent.[18] This itself would still give the BBC an impressive average weekly audience of 13.5 million – which would be far higher at moments of crisis such as in August 1991. More recently, the BBC has been able to conduct its own audience research in the Soviet Union. In 1990, a survey of Moscow, Leningrad and Kiev found that 6 per cent of the adult population over 18 (i.e. about 720,000 people) listened to the BBC Russian Service. The corresponding figure for VOA was 7.7 per cent and for Radio Liberty, 5.4 per cent.[19] The results are not necessarily representative of the USSR as a whole because they over-represent the educated and urbanized sections of the population. However, given the political importance of these three cities, the size of this BBC audience is obviously significant.

The relevance of the BBC
It is likely, in the present climate in the former USSR, that listening to foreign radio will fluctuate and will reach peak levels only in times of crisis. However, it is impossible to measure the importance of a foreign station merely by its current audience ratings. Each of the main Western stations broadcasting to the USSR has had its own distinctive principles and purposes – and the Soviet listener knew this very well. The Voice of America is essentially the voice of a superpower. Radio Liberty traditionally set out to serve as a substitute for the opposition in the USSR; and much of its popular appeal lay in its heavy coverage of Soviet domestic affairs.

The reputation of the BBC World Service stems from a different tradition. First, it enjoys a genuine editorial independence from government (unlike practically all other foreign stations). Secondly (unlike Radio Liberty), it did not cater only for communist countries, and seeks to provide its audience with a worldwide perspective. Thirdly, it has evolved a certain brand of political impartiality which may have been easier to recognize than to define. This was not inconsistent, during the cold war years, with the broadcasting of extremely negative material about the Soviet Union. (For example, the BBC Russian Service in the 1970s gave marathon coverage to the writings of Alexander Solzhenitsyn.) 'Impartiality' effectively means that the BBC has no corporate political views of its own but acts as the publisher, not the author, of the opinions it broadcasts. It reflects the prevalent views of the day, including of course the views prevalent in Britain. It also reflects minority views and the views of opposition parties.

This BBC approach did not invariably give listeners in the former USSR all that they wanted. In January 1991, for example, listeners in Lithuania said they would have preferred greater BBC coverage of the crisis in their own country and less on the Gulf war, which was then in progress.[20] Furthermore, the BBC style of impartiality was sometimes bitterly criticized. A prominent Soviet dissident, the late Andrei Amalrik, complained that the BBC output showed 'a certain wishy-washiness: on the one hand ... on the other ... I suppose that is how the British are'. Solzhenitsyn, when he visited the BBC in 1976, strongly objected to the style of the BBC Russian Service commentator, the late Anatol Goldberg, whose approach, he complained, was no better than 'water trickling through your fingers'.[21] Goldberg, who regularly broadcast in Russian (usually several times a week) from the late 1940s until his death in 1982, was at that time the best-known voice of the BBC Russian Service.

Yet, despite the intermittent criticism, it remains true that the BBC established its own distinct reputation with its Soviet audience – which some listeners may not have liked, but which many others enormously appreciated. Only with the advent of openness did it become possible, through interviews on the spot, to establish this fact. As one BBC listener in Moscow recently told me: 'The uniqueness of Goldberg was that he destroyed the "enemy image". He taught us – or me at any rate – to see Britain not as a potential enemy but as a society made up of people who, like us, just want to live and who are trying to understand us.' 'The whole country listened to him', so I was told by one of Russia's leading sociologists, Professor Yury Levada. And one of the pioneers of public opinion research in the USSR, Professor Boris Grushin of Moscow University, said very much the same thing. Although not a regular BBC listener, as he explained, he was in no doubt as to Goldberg's reputation: 'He was extraordinarily popular. He was the Number One. And the main reason for the great impact he made was his realism... He never made any opinionated judgments ... of a kind which were and still are made by a great many journalists in order to increase their audience and win cheap popularity.' Grushin added that in his view the role of the BBC during the 1960s and 1970s was 'more powerful than that of all the other radio stations', probably because the BBC 'provided information which was less "ideological"' than that of other Western stations.[22] Another former listener, the former KGB agent Oleg Gordievsky, was also full of praise: 'It is impossible to overestimate the importance of the BBC in the Soviet Union. You were like a university to us.'[23]

All in all it is not difficult to show the enormous impact which the West has made on Russia. And the evidence just quoted indicates, in particular, that the BBC has provided listeners in the ex-Soviet Union with a type of information which has not been available to them from anywhere else.

The impact of Soviet glasnost on the outside world

The impact of the West on the former USSR may seem obvious enough. When it comes to the other side of the coin – the effect of glasnost or openness on the West – the matter is less simple. Many people, including perhaps some Russians, might argue that Russia has infinitely more to learn from the West than to offer. It can also be argued with considerable persuasive force that the cold war did not end in compromise or 'convergence' between the two systems, but in a more or less outright Western victory. Of course, the ending of the cold war itself is bound to have an impact on the West. But this – so it might again be argued – was due to the collapse of communism and not, in any true sense, to Soviet influence.

Yet, all the same, it would be impossible to deny that during the late 1980s, at least, the then Soviet leadership seized the international initiative, dominated the world agenda in a positive way and won respect in the outside world to a greater extent, probably, more than had been the case at any time in Soviet history. That in turn made a major impact on the intellectual climate in the West – an impact which, paradoxically enough, preceded and did not follow the end of the cold war.

The international impact of Gorbachev

In order to see this, one has only to recall the origins of Western 'Gorbymania' – as reflected in opinion polls and in other evidence of the 1980s. In July 1989, when Gorbachev paid a visit to West Germany, he got a public welcome which at times seemed little short of delirious: no world leader had ever been so popular among West Germans, according to a poll conducted by the magazine *Der Spiegel*.[24] At that time, of course, the Berlin Wall was still standing and there was not even a promise from Moscow to accept the reunification of Germany.

The impact of Gorbachev and his 'new thinking' was similarly visible (to varying degrees) in other Western countries. Thus, according to a British opinion poll of January 1985, 62 per cent of those interviewed said that they disapproved of Russia's role in world affairs; by January 1988, this figure had fallen to 30 per cent; and in another British poll, of February 1989, as many as 79 per cent of the sample said they had a good opinion of Gorbachev.[25] Meanwhile in November 1987, *The Mail on Sunday* had published serial extracts from Gorbachev's new book *Perestroika*.[26] This itself reflected a change of climate – because the serialization in a major British newspaper of a book by, say, Brezhnev, or any previous Soviet leader, would have been virtually unthinkable. A similar change was becoming visible in the United States. A poll of December 1987 found that as many as 65 per cent of Americans interviewed said they had a favourable view of Gorbachev; in this particular poll only 61 per cent professed a similarly favourable view of Ronald Reagan.[27]

The significant thing about these examples, for our purposes, is their date. Up until 1989 the cold war – in 'objective' terms – was still very much in being. The truth about Stalin had barely been revealed to the Soviet public, and Europe was still divided. The Gorbachev leadership in 1987 had said a good deal about reform, but had achieved very little.

But if 'Gorbymania' preceded, and did not follow, the end of the cold war, how is this to be explained? No doubt certain Western leaders, notably Mrs Thatcher, played a part in creating a more positive attitude towards the new Soviet leaders. But one could also suggest two other factors. First, Soviet glasnost was beginning to undermine the conventional Western stereotype of Soviet politics. Second, the Western media (unintentionally perhaps) played a major role in this change of Western perceptions.

For many years prior to 1985, the Kremlin had been regarded in the Western world with a large measure of cynicism – as a corrupt gerontocracy, motivated primarily by a desire to preserve its own power at home and by expansionist aims abroad. The regime's secrecy was seen as a major reason for distrust; and the prospects for negotiating any fundamental East-West settlement were thought to be negligible. But glasnost – even in its early period – steadily began to throw doubt on that picture. The accession to power of Gorbachev and his advisers immediately destroyed the image of a gerontocratic, or undynamic, leadership. Their later extension of openness, as well as their gradual repudiation of the 'enemy image' of the West, also seems to have had an impact abroad. The Western public became increasingly unwilling to assume as a matter of course that the new Soviet leadership was insincere. A *Newsweek* poll of December 1987 captured the American mood very succinctly: it found that 50 per cent of those interviewed thought Gorbachev wanted peace, as against 39 per cent who believed he was merely trying to create a good public image.[28]

Gorbachev's impact on public opinion in the West was itself enough to increase his international leverage. But it was due to more than just 'public relations' and seems to have been based on something of an intellectual challenge. For one thing, by progressively removing the sense of threat which had united the Western alliance for the preceding 40 years, he and his colleagues made it necessary for the West to start reappraising its own fundamental goals, interests and priorities. For another, the advent of glasnost involved an element of surprise which caught the West unprepared. The crisis of the Soviet system had, it is true, been (correctly) foreseen by many in the West for some time. But the manner in which reform began was almost entirely unexpected. Few had imagined that reform would be launched from above – by people like Gorbachev, Shevardnadze or indeed Yeltsin, all of whom in their time had applauded the speeches of Leonid Brezhnev. Indeed, some Western experts may have found this harder to understand than many members of the Western public.

Finally, it seems that the Western media also contributed to the impact of Soviet glasnost on the West – even though many newspapers were editorially sceptical about Gorbachev. That explanation makes sense in several ways. After 1985, the Soviet Union and its leadership all of a sudden became a journalistically interesting story for the Western media. Its new leader was able to use this opportunity to get his message directly across to the world at large. Thanks to television, millions of Western viewers saw him and formed their own first-hand impressions, which were sometimes more favourable than those of the experts. This, if it proves nothing else, at least illustrates the growing importance of international television in helping the public to reach more informed judgments on foreign affairs.

Russian openness and the climate in the West
But the international effect of Russian openness went considerably beyond the personal impact of Gorbachev. The fact that the former USSR was no longer a closed society had major consequences for the Western political climate. Even to mention this fact is to open up a vast and speculative subject, which cannot adequately be dealt with in a short space. Yet the subject is too important to leave out of account. And one way of approaching it is to consider not so much the future, but the impact which the cold war and Soviet secrecy made on the Western world in the past.

One obvious fact is that worst-case scenarios were the subject of endless debate. By no means all of them were unfounded. The danger and likely consequences of a nuclear attack were widely discussed, not least in the early 1980s. So also were the danger and likely consequences of a hypothetical Soviet victory over the West. To appreciate the atmosphere of earlier days, one has only to reread part of the interview given by Alexander Solzhenitsyn to BBC television on 1 March 1976:

> I would like to make myself clear. The situation at the moment is
> such – the Soviet Union's economy is on such a war footing – that
> even if it were the unanimous opinion of all the members of the
> Politburo not to start a war, this would no longer be in their power …
> The situation now is such that one must think not of what might
> happen unexpectedly in the Soviet Union – because in the Soviet

Union nothing will happen unexpectedly. One must think of what might happen unexpectedly in the West. The West is on the verge of a collapse created by its own hands ...[29]

Warnings such as these had an enormous international impact. They are of interest today not because they proved mistaken (much of what Solzhenitsyn said about the then Soviet regime has been confirmed) but because they demonstrate the difficulties of the pre-glasnost era. At that time, there was no reliable information against which the validity of such warnings could be tested, either one way or the other. And one could quote even more horrendous scenarios from the literature of the cold war years – sometimes from highly professional experts. The following scenario of the consequences of an American surrender to the communist powers is just one example. It comes from a book entitled *The Question of National Defense*, written by a professor at Princeton University and published in 1959:

No one can say reliably what the enemy would impose upon this country if it were to surrender without fighting. But some lines of this dismal picture can be drawn and dismal it would be, indeed ... The government would go over into the hands of Communist trustees ... Perhaps 100,000,000 or 200,000,000 Chinese would be moved to this country, taking over the houses we inhabit now. According to their standards, even when crammed together with us, they would be better off than they are now. Our factories would produce 'reparations' for the rest of the world ... Or perhaps the new masters would find it better to dismantle the factories and have them shipped to the underdeveloped countries of Asia and Africa ...[30]

This picture, coming as it did from an academic, illuminates, as well as anything can, the depths of fear which the perception of a communist threat aroused. But, here again, lack of information made testing impossible. Indeed, the scenario at that time had a certain plausibility. Proponents of the 'worst case' could argue that communist rule – like that of the Nazis – had proved to be far more ruthless than many had expected.

The worst-case approach is, of course, an inherent tendency when estimating the military power of an adversary in the absence of reliable information. In this context, it is worth quoting a comment made by an intelligence specialist, Michael Herman, on the attitudes underlying military intelligence:

> Where ideology provides some of the adrenalin there is a special temptation to dramatize the strength of 'the enemy'. This reinforces the legitimate role of threat detection. Most practitioners have a self-image in the professional subconscious of themselves as warners, sounding the tocsin and jolting others out of their complacency. Support of one's national forces adds its own emotional overtones … On the whole, it is more satisfying, safer professionally, and easier to live with oneself and one's colleagues as a hawk than as a wimp.[31]

Worst-case thinking is far less relevant now than it once was. This is, of course, due not just to openness but to the climate of trust created by the ending of the cold war. Nevertheless Soviet openness had a powerful accelerating effect in creating this new climate of trust.

One of the earliest results of glasnost in the 1980s was a change in the intellectual climate in the USSR – and this was bound to have repercussions abroad. It was a process which might be described as 'de-Orwellianization'. One of its results was to overturn the old Western assumption that nothing in Soviet politics could be accepted at face value; therefore the traditional 'Kremlinological' techniques became obsolete. Normal political dialogue between citizens of the USSR and foreigners became an established fact. One further result of 'de-Orwellianization' was that the whole perception in the West of the Russian leaders as people 'totally unlike us' lost much of its force. Today's Russian leaders are committed, in principle at least, to the ideas of a rule of law, as well as to multi-party democracy. The most important thing, however, is that as a direct result of the new openness, Russian motivations can now be studied empirically, through normal information channels, in much the same way as one can study the motivations of other countries.

Openness could have other consequences, too, for the Western political climate. In the past Western policies towards the then USSR were, for reasons already mentioned, based to a considerable extent on secret information. Freer access to information could make it easier for individuals or groups outside government to challenge official policies or versions of events. From that point of view, openness might possibly have the effect of 'democratizing' future foreign policy debates. Regardless, however, of what policies are eventually adopted by the outside world towards the former Soviet Union, there are grounds for thinking that future debates – and future choices – in this area will be far better informed than they ever were in the past.

It has been argued in this chapter that Russian openness has indeed been a two-way process, even though not a symmetrical one. After six years of 'glasnost', the Soviet Union lost its ideology, with sometimes traumatic side-effects, and then disintegrated. That in turn deprived the West of its main adversary, with consequences which may themselves be far-reaching. The advent of openness was by no means the only reason for these fundamental changes, but it was a powerful accelerating factor.

However, that is not quite the end of the story where information and the media are concerned. For it was not just a question of the media helping to destroy the Iron Curtain and end the cold war. It is equally true that the disappearance of the Iron Curtain, once complete, will create new opportunities – and may pose new problems – for the international information system itself. This is the subject with which the following chapter will be concerned.

7

A MORE OPEN WORLD: PROBLEMS AND PROSPECTS

To return to the more immediate present and assuming that openness in Russia and the ex-Soviet Union has come to stay, what are the likely implications for the international media and the international transmission of information? The control of information will, by definition, become increasingly 'demonopolized'; and this will give the ordinary citizen a wider range of choice. Apart from that, I shall suggest at least three actual or potential consequences of Russian openness for the outside world – some of which overlap. They are:

(1) An acceleration of the development of the international media which is already under way. Russia is now close to becoming integrated into the world mass communication network. This will, among other things, add a fresh importance to the role of international public service broadcasting by the BBC World Service in the decades ahead.

(2) An increase in the relative importance of public as opposed to secret information in policy-making. This, among other things, will raise issues about the role and public funding of Russian or related regional studies in Britain; and

(3) A greatly reduced preoccupation with deterrence, if the political climate in the West changes in the way discussed in the last chapter; and

an increased public concern with what is currently called 'soft power' as opposed to 'hard power' in international relations. This itself could provide new scope for the international media; and it could provide an opportunity, in Russia and elsewhere, to strengthen media freedom within a framework of international law.

Some possible snags

None of this is intended to suggest that openness in itself will be a panacea. The development of contacts, and the free flow of information, between Russia and the West could well be impeded by other difficulties; and these are likely to be of at least three different kinds.

The first difficulty, as already pointed out, is that of *rising costs*. To an increasing extent, the obstacles to the movement of people and ideas across frontiers are likely to be economic or commercial, rather than ideological as in the past. There may well be a choice which has to be made between state-controlled and subsidized information, which is cheap, and commercially provided information, which is expensive. Recent developments in Russia highlight this problem. The rise in the price of Russian books and newspapers, as the country moves towards the market, will certainly cause financial problems for universities in the West (unless or until Russian prices are stabilized). There have been reports of foreign journalists in Russia being charged exorbitant sums in hard currency in return for news stories. Sometimes the difficulties can be extreme, as the following example may show. In 1989 a public opinion research institute in Moscow began to publish a regular bulletin of its findings which was freely on offer for sale abroad. Prior to glasnost this would have been unthinkable. However, the institute had, not untypically, suffered a cut in its state subsidy. In order to help balance its budget, it therefore proposed to charge foreign subscribers an annual subscription rate of US $2,000, far above the Western market price and far beyond what most universities could afford. (After some negotiation the price was substantially lowered.) In other words 'freedom of information' means only too often that information is becoming much more expensive.

Commercial barriers can operate on both sides. One recently reported case of a British restriction related to the BBC series 'The Second Russian Revolution', transmitted in 1991, which broke entirely new ground because it included interviews with former members of the Communist Party Politburo. The series was praised in the Soviet press, but Soviet television was originally unable to show it to its own audience because it was unable to pay the hard currency demanded by the BBC. Only some months later was it eventually shown, thanks to the sponsorship of an American pharmaceutical firm, which interspersed the programme with advertisements for its own products.[1] One could quote many other cases where Russian/Western contacts are hampered by economics. Russia's foreign currency shortage imposes severe limitations on the import of foreign books and publications. It also restricts the opportunities for Russian citizens to go abroad.

A second and related obstacle to contacts and the free flow of information is that of *funding*. Western funding for East-West contacts – through broadcasting, cultural ties and Soviet studies – has come partly from government. It has been motivated, at least subconsciously, by strategic considerations, that is, by the perception of the USSR as a potential enemy. The decline of the belief in a Russian threat, as well as the fact that the former USSR is no longer a closed society, could conceivably reduce that funding over time, particularly in a climate of government budget-cutting. Furthermore, the absence of an East-West crisis could lead to a lessening of interest in Russia among the Western public. That in turn could make it harder to fund Russian studies from private sources.

Finally, a third obstacle might be described by the term *fragmentation*. Media openness and access to information do not automatically lead to greater cohesion, either within societies or between them. The notion that all conflict is essentially due to ignorance finds less favour today than it once did. And, in any case, the enlargement of media choice can have a divisive, not a unifying, effect – where, for example, an audience is fragmented among dozens of different TV channels and has no basis of common knowledge. Furthermore, domestic mass audiences tend to be interested in entertainment rather than in politics, and in home news rather than in international affairs, except in times of crisis. Pollsters, psephologists and market researchers are constantly pointing this out. Lastly, it has also emerged from research that the public in Western societies (and no doubt in other societies too) will frequently be unaware of easily available information.[2] (To take one of many examples: in a survey in America in late 1985, a startling 76 per cent of the sample was unable to name Mikhail Gorbachev as the top Soviet leader.[3]) Whatever the reason for this ignorance may be, it cannot be the result of censorship.

The possible results of openness

Nevertheless, after all due allowance for these drawbacks has been made, it is impossible to deny that the international consequences of Russian openness could – potentially – be enormous. There may be nothing inevitable about these consequences. They are important not because they are bound to transform international relations but simply because they increase the range of choices open to the outside world. It is from this angle that we now return to the possible results of openness which were listed earlier.

The international media

The steady advance of the international revolution in communications has already been discussed in Chapter 4. It has progressed further than many foresaw even 20 years ago; and the ending of the cold war has given it a new and unexpected importance.

In 1971, when the cold war was far from over, the late Alastair Buchan delivered a lecture at Essex University on the subject of *Conflict and Communication*[4] which specifically examined the international dimensions of the media, and which makes a useful benchmark for the present. His conclusions, not surprisingly for that time, were in a low key. Mechanical communications as an instrument of international peace, he argued, 'have at best proved to be double-edged weapons'. Radio had frequently been used as an instrument of war 'for purposes of international propaganda, persuasion or subversion'. By and large, he said, the growth of communications in national hands had merely 'helped keep the world fragmented by stressing national, at the expense of common, interests'. And towards the end of the lecture he observed:

> Unfortunately modern communications are not a democratic force in relations between countries but an elitist one. For structural reasons there is no question of people speaking to people … the handling of the mass media is not a democratic process. To this

drawback, the Communist powers have added a second one, an insistence that virtually all communications with them be conducted through government ... So when writers like Marshal McLuhan talk of the 'global village' they are only describing half the world.

The control of the media by elites still continues. It also remains true, as Buchan observed, that many third-world countries resist the influence of the Western media because they 'fear a return to domination by the West, neo-colonialism'. But, with the advent of Russian openness, the obstacles to a 'global village' have been gigantically reduced.

Furthermore, Buchan seriously overrated the power of governments to keep out unwelcome information from abroad. This was particularly apparent from what he said about international television and cassette recordings. He admitted to being 'dubious about the technology' of satellite television and 'even more dubious' as to whether governments would ever embark on it. The whole tone of his remarks on this subject was decidedly sceptical:

> True, we do have transnational arrangements like Eurovision, but it is is still the national authority who decides what programmes shall be transmitted. True, we may have a system of cassettes in a few years' time but the consumer's choice is likely to remain limited and largely national.

These predictions turn out to have been very wide of the mark (as shown by the conclusions of the Peacock committee quoted in Chapter 4). Neither television, nor cassettes, are any longer under the totally effective control of national governments. And what is true of the West is also beginning to come true of the former USSR. Russia is indeed becoming part of the international media network; and the intrusion of CNN television into Russia in 1991 could be a portent for the future.

It is always difficult to predict how fast the media will develop. But they have often developed faster than expected. For example, the Second World War saw an enormous expansion of international broadcasting. Yet it had been largely unforeseen by the British government which, in 1938, had apparently thought that the BBC would have to be closed down altogether, should war break out.[5] And there are now solid grounds for believing that, in the years ahead, television across frontiers will steadily expand. It will no doubt be a long time before international television becomes universally accessible; therefore, for the foreseeable future, international radio will continue to be important. But it is clear in any case that the era of foreign radio broadcasting to closed societies is giving way to an era of international broadcasting, by both radio and television, between increasingly open societies. The consequences, if this trend continues, could be enormous – for the whole world as well as for the former Soviet Union.

Russia has become exposed to the influence of the outside world at a time when the international media system is itself going through a period of rapid change. The benefits for Russia are obvious; but so are the problems. Russia has been, or will be, thrown open almost without discrimination to foreign 'mass culture' of all kinds, most of it commercially dominated. We have already noted the legal and practical difficulties of regulating the international media. In any case, legal regulation by itself can never be enough to achieve the positive aim of good-quality programmes. In the years ahead, therefore, the international airwaves could increasingly be dominated by radio or television stations of uneven quality, to put it mildly.

This once again highlights the importance of international public service broadcasting. The Russian listener or viewer, faced with a mass of not always reliable information, could have reason to be grateful for at least one source of untendentious information which he can trust. And it is here that Britain could perform a special role, certainly into the next century – thanks to the already established reputation of the BBC World Service.

The BBC's reputation in Russia has already been documented. To an important degree it stems from the traditions of the BBC World Service as a whole. No other international station of comparable importance enjoys the same freedom from both governmental and commercial control, or from the influence of political pressure groups. It has evolved principles of impartiality and factual accuracy which are praised by many but practised by few. It has a record of successful broadcasting not only to closed but to open societies: therefore it does not lose its relevance in a post-cold war world. For much of the time its programmes are followed only by a minority in a given country. But – and this is one of the BBC's traditional strengths – its audience will dramatically increase in times of crisis. Provided, of course, that the BBC maintains its traditional values in the years ahead, its international role will be enormous.

All this has a particular relevance to Russia, and none of it is very controversial. But it does require conscious policy choices. They will soon become urgent – because the BBC Charter expires in 1996. In the years after that the World Service should be not only preserved but protected against the danger of falling behind its international competitors. It should, in particular, be enabled to hold its own in the field of international television broadcasting. During the years of public expenditure cuts, the difficulties faced by the World Service were seldom due to hostility: they were simply due to lack of money, made worse by the fact that the World Service is not something over which votes are won at general elections. Therefore, a public consensus in favour of a secure if limited funding for the World Service could be of great importance not only for Britain but for the former USSR in the next century.

Public versus secret information

It followed almost by definition from glasnost that more information about Russia or the ex-USSR would come into the public domain; and that the relative importance of secret information would therefore decline. Even before the break-up of the Soviet Union, this was beginning to happen. For example, the existence of open debate in Soviet politics was making it far easier for foreign observers to assess the various lobbies with which the Soviet government was having to contend. Thus, during the Gulf crisis of 1990-91, the existence of a Soviet lobby opposed to military action against Iraq was public knowledge. On one occasion the conservative 'Soyuz' group in the Supreme Soviet claimed that the government had no constitutional right to vote at the UN for the use of military force, without first getting the approval of the Supreme Soviet itself.[6] The Soviet media reflected both sides of the debate: for example, one prominent editor maintained that it was 'no mystery' as to 'why the colonels so passionately defend Iraq'. The reason was that Iraq 'was the main buyer of our arms and the main user of our military advisers who were handsomely paid'.[7] In earlier times, Soviet internal debates would have been a closely guarded secret – which the outside world would not have known about, or would have known about only through Western intelligence sources, or perhaps through the tentative insights of Kremlinologists.

But Russian openness has also created new problems for outsiders trying to study the country. In the past, most of the difficulty of following Soviet affairs was due to information gaps in vitally important areas. One of the main difficulties today is the monitoring and processing of an often unmanageable flow of new, valuable information. One result in the West has been to revive the debate about the role and working methods of the intelligence services. The clandestine methods on which they previously relied in order to get hold of the adversary's secrets are now less relevant than they used to be. But if the flow of non-secret information from Russia continues to increase, this naturally leads on to the wider question: how is this new information flow going to be handled?

In 1986, over 8,500 newspapers and over 1,500 magazines or journals were published in the USSR.[8] Many were unavailable to foreign subscribers, but their prices were usually low. Being subject to censorship, they all pursued a virtually identical political line. In a sense, this made the job of a foreign diplomat or expert relatively easy – because it was possible to deduce current tendencies by reading only a very small selection of the sample. But today it is far harder to follow events in the former USSR by relying on a small selection of newspapers. Thousands of entirely new publications of unprecedented diversity are appearing (in 1991 alone some 1,700 new independent newspapers were registered in Russia).[9] Many of them are bound to contain material of significance to the outside world – about new political leaders, the programmes of new political parties, recent legislation and much else.

To follow all of the post-censorship literature in the former USSR would be a full-time job for a large team; and would require a knowledge not just of Russian but of a number of other languages. At present, the most systematic day-by-day coverage of Soviet events is the coverage provided by the BBC Monitoring Service at Caversham and the American Foreign Broadcasting Information Service (FBIS), based in Reston, Virginia, as well as by the Radio Free Europe/Radio Liberty Research Institute in Munich, which has a library of 120,000 books and a collection of some 3 million information items on the former USSR.[10] Much of this could presumably become obsolete unless constantly updated. But the pace of change in the former USSR raises yet again a question which has been repeatedly aired in the past: namely, the future of Russian studies in Britain. Their decline after the early 1970s was a matter of more or less common knowledge.

Between the early 1970s and the mid-1980s the number of schools in the United Kingdom teaching Russian fell by half (from about 800 to under 400). Soviet studies in British universities, which had expanded after the Second World War, suffered a decisive reversal after 1979 with the closing of a number of Russian-based courses owing to financial constraints. This led not only to fears of a 'brain drain' of Soviet experts to the United States, but to the risk of the erosion of Soviet expertise through the retirement of the older generation of experts.[11] A government-commissioned inquiry into the state of Russian and East European studies in Britain later recommended the setting up of ten new university lectureships for at least eight years; and proposed government funding for these studies to the amount of £9.5 million spread over fourteen years (with a sharp drop thereafter).[12] But government funding to date has fallen a good deal below this seemingly modest figure.[13]

In 1986 a report by the House of Commons Foreign Affairs Committee on UK-Soviet relations expressed fears that the Foreign and Commonwealth Office Research Department itself might 'find difficulty in obtaining information, or even recruiting sufficiently qualified staff, if the erosion of the university base continues'.[14] The warning seems as valid today as it was then. Meanwhile, in 1990, Sir Bryan Cartledge, a former British ambassador to the Soviet Union, expressed concern that 'if the situation ... does not change, and quickly, a whole field of learning and intellectual activity ... will be the monopoly of ... the US, France and Germany'.[15]

It is undoubtedly true that the problems of studying a post-communist Russia will be substantially different from those of the traditional sovietology.[16] But the study will surely be needed, if only because of Russia's enormous importance as a world power. It is, of course, never easy to demonstrate the 'usefulness' of information about a region; but. one historical detail may perhaps be worth mentioning. Until 1917, Lenin was largely unknown even in his own country. However, as early as 1910 he had earned a short mention in the current edition of the *Cambridge Modern History*.[17] One can never be sure when information will later become valuable.

A *more open world: problems and prospects*

Hard power versus soft power

From all that has just been said, both in this chapter and in Chapter 6, a further consequence could follow for the West – with a potential relevance to the flow of information and the media. The perennial debate about 'deterrence' could recede – not because the debate has been resolved but because it has lost its immediacy. Already there seems to be some intellectual recognition of this fact. Hence the distinction between 'hard power' and 'soft power' recently put forward by Professor Robert Nye of Harvard University (who believes in both). As Nye defined it:

> Hard power is based on military and economic might. Soft power, the ability to coopt rather than command, rests on intangible resources: culture, ideology, the ability to use international institutions to determine the framework of debate.[18]

There may be better terms (such as 'influence' or 'persuasion') which make the same point. But the underlying idea – that there are some things in politics which cannot be achieved by military or economic power alone – is of great importance.

In this context, Russia's recent interest in establishing a rule of law – including a legally guaranteed media freedom – becomes particularly important. Moscow, as already noted in Chapter 4, has shown a strong interest in joining the Council of Europe; and there seems every reason why Russia should be encouraged to qualify for membership. If that were to happen in the not too distant future, it would give the outside world an effective as well as a constructive influence on the strengthening of media freedom in Russia (to an extent which was impossible during the cold war era). The admission of new member states to the Council of Europe is not just a formality: it depends on the applicants satisfying fairly rigorous human rights criteria. On the other hand, it is less complex than, for instance, the admission of new members to military or economic alliances (such as NATO and the EC). If Russia were to join the Council, this would have at least one result of enormous importance. The Council, as already noted, has a court with supranational jurisdiction where individuals can, in certain conditions, find a remedy of last resort. If Russia belonged to the Council, the territory over which the Court had jurisdiction would of course be vastly extended; and a start could be made in creating a body of legal principles (covering press freedom and freedom of information, among other things) which would be common both to the West and to much of the former communist world. If the Council of Europe were indeed to extend its jurisdiction over these countries, it would, of course, face a formidable task – if only because of disputes over national minority rights in the territories of the now dissolved Soviet Union. But the task could still be worth while – since the protection of such rights requires not only the skills of politicians, but the gradual development of an accepted framework of law.

The extension of the role of international law is only one specific example of reliance on 'soft power'. More generally, the term should not be confused with 'soft sell', public relations or manipulation. What I have in mind here is the ability to command public respect, and win public support for political goals, by non-threatening, non-fraudulent and non-opportunistic means; and this is something which not even the most hard-headed politicians can afford to ignore. The celebrated question which Stalin once asked, 'The Pope! How many divisions has *he* got?' has acquired an unexpectedly ironic significance in the light of subsequent events.[19] Indeed, the whole of Soviet history from 1917 to the mid-1980s could be treated as a case-study in the exercise of 'hard power' – and as proof that 'hard power', taken by itself, is not enough to achieve policy goals. Conversely, the Gorbachev era up to the late 1980s could make a possible case-study in the use of 'soft power'. Glasnost itself seems to have been intended as an instrument of 'soft power'. Its failures (at least from Gorbachev's point of view) are only too well known. But its initial successes – as a lever of political reform – were undeniable. Equally important was Gorbachev's reliance on the Western media during the 1980s in gaining the sympathy of Western public opinion.

Soft power, in the sense discussed above, need not presuppose an adversary relationship. It implicitly recognizes the fact that political settlements not based on consent are liable, sooner or later, to unravel. At the same time, it is not inconsistent with what was written in the past about deterrence. One has only to recall an observation made in 1960 by Thomas Schelling, one of the best-known theoreticians of deterrence, that '"winning" in a conflict does not have a strictly competitive meaning; it is not winning relative to one's adversary. It means gaining relative to one's own value system'.[20]

A more open world: problems and prospects

Today – when the East-West power struggle has become a thing of the past – this dictum has acquired a totally new relevance. In June 1991, in a speech delivered in Berlin, the American Secretary of State, James Baker, put forward an idea which could, in theory, mark a revolution in international relations. He set out the objective of 'a Euro-Atlantic Community that extends east from Vancouver to Vladivostok', adding that the new architecture 'will be incomplete as long as the USSR hesitates outside'. In a sentence which seemed to question the whole traditional idea of peace through a balance of power, he concluded: 'The time has come to set new goals, which go beyond the concept of balance, and begin to establish the basis for a real cooperative security.'[21] The speech was shortly afterwards described by an American commentator as 'potentially the most important American policy statement since the cold war began'.[22]

The decline of Soviet and Russian secrecy, the appearance of an integrated world information system and the increased reliance on soft power are, it could be argued, mutually connected aspects of a broader process. One point may, however, be important enough to bear repetition. Today, Russia has become integrated in the world media system to a far greater extent that at any time in its history. In this sense, progress towards a more open world has almost certainly become an accomplished fact.

8

CONCLUSION: OPENNESS AND THE FUTURE

Already by 1990, the expressions 'post-communist' or 'post-totalitarian' had become a well-established part of commentators' vocabulary when describing the era into which the world is now entering. Few people, if any, have paused to ask why no one ever talked about the 'post-Nazi' era when describing the world after 1945. The reason, of course, is that the collapse of Germany and its allies did not give rise to any ideological or military power vacuum. As far as the West was concerned, the question 'What follows Hitler?' did not arise. The goal of building or re-establishing democracy in Western Europe was too obvious to require discussion.

In August 1991, when the Russian government formally repudiated communism, following the failure of the first *coup d'état* since 1917, the prospect of a vacuum was only too real. It became difficult to make meaningful predictions more than a few hours ahead; and even the most circumspect author was in grave danger of trying to answer what could turn out to be yesterday's questions. In discussing the international consequences of Soviet glasnost (the term itself has become superseded), it is probably more useful to take a long-term view. It is better, instead of trying to predict what will happen in the next year or two, to ask where the successor states of the USSR are likely to be at the end of the century.

What implications are the changes likely to have, so far as openness and the media are concerned?

Much has recently been said about the 'disintegration' or 'death throes' of the Soviet empire. Yet even this should be put into some perspective. It is not irrelevant to recall that when Britain relinquished its colonial empire after 1945, it lost some 98 per cent of the territory it had directly ruled. France, whose empire had been slightly smaller, lost 90 per cent of the territory which it had previously controlled.[1] Both countries survived as significant world powers, decolonization notwithstanding. The position of the former USSR is rather different. Russia, taken on its own, comprises some three-quarters of the empire's territory. Given Russia's sheer size, its geographical position, its enormous untapped natural resources and, of course, its nuclear weapons, its long-term survival as a major power is hardly in doubt.

The crucial issue is not whether Russia survives but whether, and how soon, the country develops as a democracy. Is there a chance of its following the road which Vaclav Havel sought to follow in the Czech and Slovak Federal Republic? Or is it more likely that the post-Gorbachev Soviet Union will suffer the same fate as the post-Tito Yugoslavia? In relation to the development of openness and media freedom, this question is of particular importance. It will be several years at least before the answer becomes clear. Only then, incidentally, will it be possible fully to assess the Gorbachev era. It is hardly fair to criticize Gorbachev's policies without seeing whether his successors are able to provide better solutions.

There is no way of knowing how quickly democracy can take root in Russia – given the fact that the country has never lived under real democracy during all its eleven centuries of statehood. It would be quite wrong to adopt a defeatist attitude on this question. At the same time, the prospects of success will be better if the danger signals are spotted in time. Few would deny that the immediate threat to political freedom comes from the economy. If that continues to get worse, it is only too easy to imagine what could then follow: rising prices, mass unemployment owing to the closure of bankrupt enterprises, civil disturbances and strikes accompanied by the possible sharpening of ethnic tensions, the declaration of a state of emergency, the temporary imposition of media censorship – and the disappearance of freedom of speech as we have come to know it.

But the economy is not the sole problem; and it is not surprising that comparisons should be made between the Russian crisis of today and the crisis of the Weimar Republic in Germany which preceded Hitler in the early 1930s. Both countries faced not only economic collapse but a deep crisis of self-confidence and self-esteem – due to a loss of territory and international status; and due also to the absence of a 'loyal opposition' with an interest in making the system work. It is in such situations that xenophobic nationalism can take root. A return to the old totalitarian type of control – with a mandatory ideology and 'unanimous' public opinion – would be virtually impossible, for reasons argued at the end of Chapter 5. But the danger of an authoritarian or populist dictatorship remains a real one – and is a serious potential threat to democratic advancement.

From the point of view of our subject, it is the development of Russian democracy – rather than the break-up of the Soviet empire or the collapse of communism – which is the key issue. In the gloomy scenario – where the country slid back into authoritarian rule – the chances of close rapprochement with the outside world would be greatly diminished. It would be impossible to integrate Russia into the international democratic community. The countries of the Baltic as well as those of Eastern Europe would be much more likely to gravitate towards the West, ostracizing Russia in practice if not in theory. This in turn could fuel Russian nationalism. In such a scenario, the Iron Curtain would have disappeared, the West might even get involved in Russia's internal conflicts, but the cultural barrier between Russia and its Western neighbours would not have been finally eliminated.

The optimistic scenario – the steady democratization of Russian society – could mean a change potentially so enormous as to amount to a revolution in international relations. If that were to happen, it would be increasingly difficult for the outside world to justify treating Russia as a country of inferior status. A democratic Russia would be far less likely to be seen by its neighbours as a potential threat to their security. The door could be opened to the eventual creation of a new type of cooperative international system of the kind envisaged by Secretary of State James Baker in his Berlin speech of June 1991. If Russia were a full part of such a system, this could provide its people with a non-utopian substitute for the now abandoned goal of full communism. Indeed a number of leading politicians have spoken on this general theme. Already in April 1989

87

Germany's Foreign Minister, Hans-Dietrich Genscher, told the Bundestag: 'Nothing is more powerful than an idea whose time has come. This is the idea of eliminating hostility from international relations ... of developing new peace structures.'[2] It was a concept of peace unmistakably different from the traditional one of 'peace through deterrence'. On a closely related topic, President Vaclav Havel told the United States Congress in 1990: 'You can help us most of all if you help the Soviet Union on its irreversible but immensely complicated road to democracy.'[3]

These, then, are two scenarios: others of course are possible. But where, in all this, do the media and the flow of information fit in? It would be false to suggest that glasnost or openness alone will determine the political future, any more than it was the sole factor in the events since 1985. All the same, several things can now be stated with a good deal of certainty.

First, the population – not only in the Soviet Union, but in a large part of the world – is now better informed, or has far greater access to. information, than ever before in history. In the United States, television has enormously enlarged the number of people who follow international affairs. In the early 1980s some 74 per cent of Americans were said to get their information about world events from television. This is partly due to what has been called the 'inadvertent' audience – consisting of people who, even though they might not actively seek news from abroad, nevertheless stay tuned to the television set when it gives such news.[4] In the Soviet Union (at least in the past) interest in international affairs, reflecting a curiosity about the non-communist world, was always higher than elsewhere,[5] and television in the former USSR is now almost universal. Listening to foreign broadcasts has been widespread, especially in times of crisis, for many years. Today it is totally legal – and the watching of foreign satellite television broadcasts now takes place on a small but significant scale. As already noted in earlier chapters, it cannot be assumed that the spreading of information is always conducive to harmony or benign in its effects. But the fact that tens of millions of people in Russia and elsewhere do have access to information not controlled by their governments is a virtually unalterable reality.

Secondly, the media – both Soviet and foreign – have now been shown not merely to have reflected events, but in some cases to have influenced them in a most direct fashion. The failed military coup of

August 1991 demonstrates this. The steadily expanding glasnost of the previous six years had transformed the political awareness of Soviet citizens beyond recognition and had made it almost unthinkable that they would passively accept a return to the past.

Thirdly, the advent of openness does not in itself provide automatic solutions, nor does it mean that the future is predetermined. Here, as we have just said, a great deal depends on the future of Russian democracy. But what does seem certain, as already pointed out, is that in the post-glasnost era, politicians and the public will be far better informed about policy choices than they were in the past, and that this is bound to affect the quality of political debate in the West as well as the East. In this sense, the political climate will have been substantially altered.

Fourthly, glasnost has been at least one important factor in the disappearance of the perceived external threat: and this applies to Russian perceptions of the West as well as vice versa. Living without enemies may not be without its problems. Today, however, the prospect of an international security system based on something other than a permanent common enemy is at least on the horizon. Future wars may always be possible; but there is a vast difference between the permanent possibility of conflicts and the existence of one permanent global conflict.

Finally, the dismantling of the Iron Curtain will, in certain areas, produce its own problems. In particular, as we have noted, there is a real danger of political barriers being replaced by economic ones. For example, the rising cost of books and newspapers could hamper Russian/Western contacts on both sides. And foreign travel by Russians is bound to be affected for economic reasons. Foreign currency shortages in the former Soviet Union, as well as Western restrictions on mass immigration, are bound to create barriers of their own.

In conclusion, it only remains to look at the possible policy implications of all these unprecedented developments. Major decisions, such as arms control or the granting of aid to Russia by the West, fall outside the scope of this paper. Nevertheless, the three proposals put forward earlier are worth reiterating.

First, a modest but assured funding for the expert study of the successor states of the USSR is a vital requirement during what is bound to be a long transitional period. Regardless of the changes which lie in store, Russia is here to stay; it will be a major factor for British policy-makers and it will therefore have to be studied. The ending of censorship has not solved the information problem, but has merely transformed it. The old problem of information gaps in vital places has given way to an unmanageable flow of new information. Language training has itself become a matter of greater urgency – if only to monitor some of the newly born newspapers. The emergence of over a dozen independent nation-states also raises the question of the study of *their* languages. To rely on the fact that most of the new national intelligentsia speak English or Russian is hardly an adequate response. Inability to read the local national press will deprive foreigners of the opportunity to form an independent judgment of what is happening. No doubt there will be a pooling of expertise among Western experts. But if Britain is to be a voice in the world, it will need to be seen to possess an independent expertise of its own.

Secondly, the appearance of a pluralistic and uncensored media in the (former) Soviet Union in no way makes the role of international public service broadcasting redundant. The new media in what was the USSR will be freer, but probably very uneven. Many of its spokesmen will have political axes to grind. Therefore the role of responsible quality journalism offering disinterested information from the outside world will increase rather than diminish. It is here that the BBC could have a part to play – by building on a tradition and reputation which is already long established. Again, the proposal in itself is hardly controversial. The sole problem is that of funding.

Thirdly, there now exists a greater opportunity than at any previous time to build an international framework of law governing media freedom, freedom of information and, of course, human rights more generally. This is a strong reason for encouraging Russia to qualify for membership of the Council of Europe in the not too distant future – because the Council (unlike other East-West forums) is equipped with judicial mechanisms for the enforcement of the principles to which it is committed.

These three proposals at least have the advantage of being relatively uncomplicated, inexpensive and free of risk. For that reason they could conceivably bring disproportionate benefits. Expert study, international public service broadcasting and the promotion of an international media and information law all have a direct relevance to what we earlier referred to as 'soft power' – something which we suggested would become increasingly important precisely because it does not presuppose an adversary relationship. As to the international impact of Soviet glasnost, it only remains to record that it was a detonator, which set off a chain reaction whose worldwide consequences will be felt for many decades to come.

NOTES

Chapter 1: Introduction

1 *The Observer*, 12 February 1961, quoted in John Strachey, *On the Prevention of War* (London: Macmillan, 1962), p. 265.

2 See, in particular, Stephen White, *Gorbachev and After* (Cambridge: Cambridge University Press, 1991), especially Chapter 3; also Alec Nove, *Glasnost' in Action: Cultural Renaissance in Russia* (Boston and London: Unwin Hyman, 1989).

3 Walter Lippmann, *Public Opinion* (1921), quoted in Wilbur Schramm and Donald F. Roberts, eds, *The Process and Effects of Mass Communication*, 2nd rev. edn (Urbana, Chicago and London: University of Illinois Press, 1971), p. 265.

4 This remark does not appear to be documented, but its authenticity was confirmed from Ralph Nader's office in Washington.

5 In 1913 there were said to be 21 copies of newspapers for every 1,000 inhabitants in the Russian empire; see *Pechat' SSSR za 50 let. Statisticheskie ocherki* (Moscow: Kniga, 1967), p. 156. By 1917, the supply of newspapers had undoubtedly dropped sharply below this level.

6 Bertrand Russell, *The Practice and Theory of Bolshevism*, 2nd edn (London: Allen and Unwin, 1949), p. 65. The first edition of the book appeared in 1920.

7 See *The Times*, 16 May 1972 (letter from Karl Nesseler, recalling how he

had been able to subscribe to the paper in Germany until August 1939).
The importation into the Reich of German-language newspapers and
journals from abroad was officially banned by the Nazis only in December
1939: see *Keesing's Contemporary Archives* (13-20 January 1940), p. 3881.

8 See the article on 'The Press and the Russian Revolution' in George
Jackson and Robert Devlin, eds, *Dictionary of the Russian Revolution*
(New York, Westport, CT, and London: The Greenwood Press, 1989),
p. 457. The information about the need for passports was given to me in a
BBC interview by the late M. Phillips Price, *Manchester Guardian*
correspondent in Russia from 1914 to 1918.

9 Bernard Pares, *Russia and the Peace* (Harmondsworth: Penguin Books,
1944), p. 183.

10 See *The History of 'The Times'*, Vol. 4 (London: *The Times*, 1952),
pp. 911-12. Soviet affairs during this period were covered by the paper's
correspondent in Riga.

11 See William Henry Chamberlin, 'Under Lenin and Stalin', *Survey* (London), No. 68, July 1968, p. 131.

12 See Klaus Mehnert, 'The Thirties and the Fifties', *Survey*, supra, p. 134.
The author had worked as a German journalist in the Soviet Union both
before and after the Second World War.

13 See 'Obozrevatel' (pseudonym), 'In the Shadow of 1947', *Survey*, supra,
pp. 158ff.

14 See Herman Poerzgen, 'Today and Yesterday', *Survey*, supra, p. 137.

15 The Soviet decision was made known to foreign correspondents on 23
March 1961, although never announced in the Soviet press: see *Keesing's
Contemporary Archives* (15-22 April 1961), p. 18033.

16 V.I. Stepakov, *Partiinoi propagande – nauchnye osnovy* (Moscow:
Politizdat, 1967), p. 71; Viktor Afanasyev, in G.L. Smirnov et al., eds,
*Problemy kompleksnogo osushchestvleniya zadach kommunisticheskogo
vospitaniya v svete reshenii XXV s'ezda KPSS* (Moscow: Politizdat, 1978),
p. 302.

17 Quoted in the Moscow mass circulation weekly *Argumenty i fakty* (hereafter *AiF*), No. 2, 1991.

18 The early history of Soviet censorship is documented in Robert Conquest,
ed., *The Politics of Ideas in the USSR* (London: Bodley Head, 1967).

19 *Izvestiya*, 3 November 1988.

20 See the interview by Yu. Feofanov in *ibid.*, 17 October 1986, where the
question of 'sub-legal acts' was raised apparently for the first time.
Subsequently, on 29 November 1990, the Soviet Committee for Constitutional Oversight, which was responsible for ensuring that laws complied

with the country's constitution, ruled that enactments affecting the rights and freedoms of citizens were invalid unless published; see *AiF*, No. 1, 1991.

21 *Izvestiya*, 1 August 1990.

22 Information provided to the author by Professor Valery Savitsky of the USSR Institute of State and Law in an interview in Moscow in June 1991.

23 See *Novyi mir* (Moscow), No. 5, 1990, p. 243.

24 See *Pravda*, 15 March 1989, for an interview with one of those responsible for the jamming operation.

25 Quoted in Dmitri Volkogonov, *Stalin: Triumph and Tragedy*, ed. and tr. Harold Shukman (London: Weidenfeld and Nicolson, 1991), p. 285.

26 See David Wedgwood Benn, *Persuasion and Soviet Politics* (Oxford: Basil Blackwell, 1989), especially Chapter 5, for a more detailed account of the criticisms of the media in Soviet writings during the Brezhnev era.

27 See *Bol'shaya sovetskaya entsiklopediya*, 3rd edn (Moscow: Sovetskaya entsiklopediya Publishing House, 1974), Vol. 18, pp. 242-3.

28 See Walter Bedell Smith, *Moscow Mission: 1946-1949* (Melbourne, London and Toronto: William Heinemann, 1950), p. 43. The dictum was that of the British correspondent Paul Winterton, who reported from Russia during the Second World War.

Chapter 2: Glasnost after 1985

1 The text of the resolution was published in *Pravda*, 5 July 1988.

2 *Pravda*, 30 March 1968. Brezhnev had then said that 'glasnost, the informing of the party masses and of all working people about the activity of the party, is a principle of our party life and we firmly follow this principle'.

3 *Konstitutsiya (Osnovnoi Zakon) Soyuza Sovetskikh Sotsialisticheskikh Respublik* (Moscow: *Pravda* Publishing House, 1977), Article 9.

4 See *Sovershenstvovanie razvitogo sotsializma i ideologicheskaya rabota partii v svete reshenii iyun'skogo (1983g.) plenuma TsK KPSS* (Moscow: Politizdat, 1985), pp. 30-1.

5 *Pravda*, 12 March 1985.

6 *Ibid.*, 27 March 1985.

7 *Ibid.*, 24 April 1985.

8 See Joshua Muravchik, 'Gorbachev, the True Communist', *The American Enterprise*, March/April 1990, pp. 40ff.

9 See *Pravda*, 15 May 1986 (Gorbachev's broadcast on Chernobyl); also Angus Roxburgh, *The Second Russian Revolution* (London: BBC Books, 1991), pp. 40-3.

10 See Aaron Trehub, 'Gorbachev Meets Soviet Writers: a *Samizdat* Account', Radio Liberty Report (Munich), No. 399/86 (23 October 1986). Excerpts from Gorbachev's remarks also appeared in Italian in *L'Unita* and *La Repubblica* on 7 October 1986.

11 See *Pravda*, 2 August 1986.

12 See *Vedomosti Verkhovnogo Soveta SSSR*, No. 37, 1986 (10 September 1986). See, for a report on these legislative plans, the *International Herald Tribune*, 16 October 1986 (Serge Schmemann).

13 *Pravda*, 21 October 1986.

14 *Ibid.*, 30 November 1986.

15 *Ibid.*, 11 December 1986.

16 *Ibid.*, 28 January 1987.

Chapter 3: Towards freedom of information

1 Andrei D. Sakharov, *Progress, Coexistence and Intellectual Freedom* (Harmondsworth: Penguin Books, 1969), pp. 61-2.

2 *Vedomosti S'yezda narodnykh deputatov SSSR i Verkhovnogo Soveta SSSR*, No. 26, 1990, pp. 690ff. The summaries of this law and of its 1992 successor are necessarily incomplete, and deal with only the main aspects of this legislation.

3 The full text appeared in *Rossiiskaya gazeta*, 8 February 1992.

4 It was first serialized in *Novyi mir*, Nos. 8-11, 1989.

5 K.G. Myalo et al., eds, *Po stranitsam samizdata* (Moscow: Molodaya gvardiya, 1990), pp. 17-18.

6 See *Dialog*, No. 17, 1990, p. 3, which reported an opinion poll on the subject. In that survey, 21.9 per cent of the sample said they favoured a return to the pre-Bolshevik political system.

7 For a report of Kalugin's original speech attacking the KGB, see *AiF*, No. 36, 1990.

8 For example, *AiF*, No. 38, 1990, reported a demand for Gorbachev's resignation made by the former legal investigator Telman Gdlyan.

9 *AiF*, No. 30, 1990.

10 *Pravda*, 2 August, 1990. (Interview with Georgy Pryakhin of the Ideological Department of the Soviet Communist Party.)

11 For a report on the court's decision, see *Moscow News*, No. 6, 1991.

12 A decree by Gorbachev attempting to demarcate the functions of radio and television between the central and republican authorities (published in *Izvestiya*, 16 July 1990) has been overtaken by the break-up of the USSR. An earlier law of 14 May 1990 had created a new offence of publicly

insulting or slandering the President of the USSR. This offence was to be punishable by fines or imprisonment (of up to 6 years, if the insult was published in the media) but applied only to deliberate insults 'expressed in an unseemly form' or to 'fabrications ... known to be false'. See *Vedomosti S'yezda narodnykh deputatov SSSR i Verkhovnogo Soveta SSSR*, No. 22, 1990, p. 487. The only person known to have been charged under this law (Valeriya Novodvorskaya) was acquitted, sentenced to two years imprisonment for the separate offence of burning the Soviet flag, but then freed after the August coup. See *The Times*, 2 March, 1991; and *Literaturnaya gazeta*, 4 September 1991.

13 The authors were Yury Baturin, Vladimir Entin and Mikhail Fedotov, who in 1991 became Russian Deputy Minister for the Press and Information.

14 The Russian law does not specifically forbid the incitement of 'racial' (as distinct from 'national') intolerance. On the other hand, it does forbid the incitement of 'class' intolerance. In these respects it differs from Article 5 of the 1990 law, already summarized in the text.

15 Under Article 37 of the 1992 law, 'erotic' material, i.e. material which seeks systematically to exploit interest in sex, cannot be sold to the public except on specially approved premises, and/or in transparent sealed packaging. 'Erotic' material must not as a rule be broadcast to the general public, except between 11 p.m. and 4 a.m.

16 *Pravda*, 17 January 1991.

17 Reported in *AiF*, No. 46, 1990.

18 Information supplied to the author in June 1991 by the Russian State Television and Radio Company.

19 The price of newsprint immediately rose more than threefold, from 424 to 1300 roubles per ton, according to *Pravda*, 9 January 1991.

20 *AiF*, No. 33, 1990.

21 *Ibid.*, No. 35, 1990.

22 *The Times*, 15 February 1992 (Bruce Clark).

23 See the BBC *Summary of World Broadcasts*, for the Soviet Union (hereafter *SWB (SU)*), 15 January 1992, quoting the Russian Minister for the Press and Information, Mikhail Poltoranin, interviewed in the Moscow newspaper *Trud* on the previous day.

24 Reuter report from Atlanta, 29 January 1992. Mr Sagalayev is deputy chairman of TV Ostankino, Russia's biggest television company.

25 *Pravda*, 5 July 1990. The rapporteur, Nikolai Kruchina, committed suicide on 26 August 1991, in the aftermath of the coup, amidst widespread rumours that he had been implicated in frauds relating to the party's assets.

26 The estimate was given to Western journalists in Moscow by Arkady

Vol'sky, a one-time adviser to Gorbachev, on 26 August 1991; see *Report on the USSR* (Radio Free Europe/Radio Liberty Research Institute, Munich), 6 September 1991, p. 80. A much higher estimate, of around 13 billion roubles, can be found in *Izvestiya*, 10 February 1992 (Vadim Belykh and Valery Rudnev); this also discussed the difficulty of locating party assets transferred to foreign banks.

27 Boris Yeltsin decreed the party's temporary suspension on Russian territory on 23 August 1991, and its final dissolution on 6 November.

28 In an appeal for help addressed to the President and State Council of the USSR, the paper said that it no longer owned even the desks on which its journalists wrote their stories: see *Pravda*, 17 September 1991.

29 See *Izvestiya*, 23 December 1991, reporting the protest; and for a more general survey including details of the withdrawal of the amendments, see Julia Wischnewsky, 'Russia: Liberal Media Criticize Democrats in Power', *Radio Free Europe/Radio Liberty Research Report*, Munich, Vol. 1, No. 2, 10 January 1992, pp. 6-11.

30 See *Literaturnaya gazeta*, 16 January 1991, which accused the troops in Vilnius of shooting 'at unarmed people'; *Moscow News*, No. 3, 1991 appeared with black borders and published a protest at the shootings from its Board of Directors.

31 For example, *Moscow News*, No. 6, 1991, published a two-page round-up of complaints about attempts to re-impose censorship.

32 S. Gurevich, ed., *Problemy informatsii v pechati* (Moscow: Mysl, 1971), p. 23.

Chapter 4: Communication across frontiers

1 Broadcast in the USSR on 31 March 1987.

2 *The Times*, 16 October 1987.

3 *Literaturnaya gazeta*, 17 April 1991; *The Times*, 27 May 1991.

4 Reported in *AiF*, No. 4, 1991.

5 *SWB (SU)*, 8 August 1989, quoting TASS in English, 31 July 1989.

6 *Pravda*, 23 October 1986.

7 The discontinuance of Soviet jamming was reported, with regard to the BBC, in the British press on 22 January 1987 and, with regard to the Voice of America, in the press on 26 May 1987. The cessation of the jamming of Radio Liberty was reported in the press on 1 and 2 December 1988. Soviet jamming of Western broadcasts to the USSR had begun in the late 1940s but had (in the case of VOA and the BBC) sometimes been selective. It had been suspended entirely between 1963 and 1968 (until the invasion of

Notes

Czechoslovakia). It was again suspended from 1973 until 1980 (following the rise of Solidarity in Poland). The jamming of Radio Liberty was continuous until 1988.

8 *Pravda*, 15 March 1989.
9 The debate in the United States over the passage of this Act is summarized in Mike Bowker and Phil Williams, *Superpower Detente: A Reappraisal* (London: Royal Institute of International Affairs/Sage Publications, 1988), pp. 160ff.
10 *SWB (SU)*, 31 August 1990, quoting TASS, 28 August 1990.
11 *Komsomol'skaya pravda*, 2 November 1989.
12 *SWB (SU)*, 3 November 1989, quoting TASS, 1 November 1989.
13 *SWB (SU)*, 5 September 1990, quoting Helsinki Radio, 22 August 1990.
14 The figures for 1981-8 do not give any breakdown of the 'socialist states'. In relation to 1989, the term refers to the member states of the Warsaw Pact together with Yugoslavia, Cuba, Outer Mongolia, Vietnam, Laos, China and North Korea.
15 See *Pravda*, 25 July 1957, 29 January 1977 and 10 August 1977, which gave the figure of over 2.6 million Soviet citizens going abroad in 1976.
16 *Statistical Abstract of the US* (Washington: US Department of Commerce, 1990), pp. 239-40.
17 Quoted in *Izvestiya*, 29 April 1991.
18 The text appeared in *Izvestiya*, 6 June 1991. An English translation was published in *SWB (SU)*, 8 June 1991.
19 For a survey of this problem, see Vera Tolz, '"Brain Drain" – The Main Problem of Soviet Science?', RFE/RL *Report on the USSR*, 28 June 1991, p. 21.
20 See the *Financial Times*, 27 January 1991 (Judy Dempsey), where this figure was attributed to a Soviet diplomat in Vienna, who added that he thought it on the high side.
21 See, for example, Walter R. Roberts and Harold E. Engle, 'The Global Information Revolution and the Communist World', *The Washington Quarterly*, Spring 1986, pp. 141ff. and sources there cited.
22 Ithiel de Sola Pool et al., eds, *Handbook of Communication* (Chicago, 1973), p. 479, quoted in Stephen White, *Political Culture and Soviet Politics* (London: Macmillan, 1979), p. 183.
23 Vladimir Yaroshenko, *'Chernyi efir'. Podryvnaya propaganda v sisteme burzhuaznogo vneshnepoliticheskogo radioveshchaniya* (Moscow: Iskusstvo, 1986), p. 192.
24 I.F. Vydrin and S.V. Myagchenkov, eds, *Vospitanie u shkol'nikov neprimiromosti k burzhuaznoi ideologii i propagande* (Moscow:

Pedagogika, 1985), p. 71.

25 *Politicheskoe obrazovanie* (Moscow), No. 10, 1987, p. 101.

26 V.P. Ostrovsky et al., eds, *Istoriya SSSR: Uchebnik dlya 11 klassa srednei shkoly* (Moscow: Prosveshchenie, 1990), p. 196.

27 See *International Herald Tribune*, 28 October 1983 (Serge Schmemann); and Ellen Mickiewicz, *Split Signals: Television and Politics in the Soviet Union* (New York and Oxford: Oxford University Press, 1988), pp. 11-13.

28 See Peter Havlik, 'Information and Related Technologies and their Impact on East-West Relations', Vienna Institute for Comparative Economic Studies, Reprint-Serie, No. 129, October 1990, p. 206.

29 *Cable and Satellite Yearbook, 1991* (London: 21st Century Publishing, 1991), pp. 57, 59.

30 *SSSR v tsifrakh v 1989 godu* (Moscow: Finansy i statistika, 1990), p. 87.

31 Mickiewicz, *Split Signals*, supra (n. 27), p. 3.

32 In 1984 a survey of schoolchildren in the Moscow area reported that 85 per cent followed current events through television, while only 14.8 per cent found political study sessions at school interesting: *Sotsiologicheskie issledovaniya*, No. 2, 1984, p. 82.

33 V.I. Ivanov et al., eds, *Sotsiologiya i propaganda* (Moscow: Nauka, 1986), p. 120.

34 Boris Firsov, in Yu. Vooglaid et al., eds, *Materialy vstrechi sotsiologov*, Vol. 1 (Tartu University, 1967), p. 78.

35 See, for the text of this Soviet draft convention, UN General Assembly document A/8771, 9 August 1972. The then Soviet view of this subject can be found in Yury Kolosov, *Massovaya informatsiya i mezhdunarodnoe pravo* (Moscow: Nauka, 1974), especially at pp. 147ff.

36 See *Cable and Satellite Yearbook, 1991*, supra (n. 29), pp. 55-9, for a country-by-country analysis of cable and satellite television in Europe.

37 See *Nation to Nation* (published by the BBC World Service,London), October 1991, p. 7. (Interview with Chris Irwin, chief executive of BBC World Service Television.) See also Chris Irwin, inaugural lecture at the Singapore Press Club, 27 September 1991 (BBC World Service).

38 *International Herald Tribune*, 15-16 February 1992 (business section).

39 For example, *Literaturnaya gazeta*, 24 July and 10 October 1991.

40 See *The Times*, 30 January 1992, 'Gallup tunes into Russia's tastes in TV' (Melinda Wittstock).

41 BBC *Monitoring Report*, 21 January 1991; *SWB (SU)*, 16 September 1991, quoting Radio Rossiya, 12 September 1991.

42 *Report of the Committee on Financing the BBC*, under the chairmanship of Professor Alan Peacock (London, HMSO, 1986, Cmnd 9824), para. 543.

Notes

43 First published in the *UN Yearbook, 1948* (New York: United Nations Publications).

44 First published in the *UN Yearbook, 1966* (New York: United Nations Publications).

45 *Conference on Security and Co-operation in Europe: Final Act* (London: HMSO, 1975, Cmnd 6198).

46 *The Independent*, 22 February 1990.

47 Shevardnadze interview in *Moscow News*, No. 9, 1990.

48 For full details, see A.H. Robertson, *Human Rights in Europe*, 2nd rev. edn (Manchester University Press, 1977). This is a standard work on the Council of Europe. Subsequently, in 1989, the Council adopted the 'European Convention on Transfrontier Television' (European Treaty Series, No. 132), aimed at promoting freedom of information and unhindered broadcasting (subject to certain programme standards) between the countries which have signed the Convention. Signatories to date include, *inter alia*, Poland, Hungary and Yugoslavia, but not the USSR or Russia.

49 International regulation at a technical level is governed by the International Telecommunication Convention of 1973; the International Telecommunications Union (ITU) is, within the UN, the body responsible in this field. See, as to the general application of international law to the media, Edward Ploman, ed., *International Law Governing Communications and Information: A Collection of Basic Documents* (London: Frances Pinter, 1982).

50 *The Times*, 30 May 1991 (Mary Dejevsky). Summaries of the earlier Soviet legislation in this area, and assessments of the problems facing foreign investors, can be found in Leonard Geron, *Soviet Foreign Economic Policy under Perestroika* (London: Royal Institute of International Affairs/Pinter Publishers, 1990); also in Margie Lindsay, *International Business in Gorbachev's Soviet Union* (London: Pinter Publishers, 1989).

51 *SSSR v tsifrakh v 1989 godu* (Moscow: Finansy i statistika, 1990), p. 33.

52 Philip Hanson, 'Joint Ventures still Expanding despite Everything', RFE/RL *Report on the USSR*, 9 August 1991, p. 6.

53 BBC World Service news release, 9 October 1991.

54 *SWB Weekly Economic Report*, 21 December 1990.

55 *International Herald Tribune*, 24 July 1991.

56 *Ibid.*, 17 February 1992.

57 See 'The lure of ink', *The Economist*, 20 April 1991.

58 *Independent on Sunday*, 20 May 1991 (Edward Steen).

59 *The Independent*, 16 May 1990 (Imre Karacs); *Financial Times*, 4 July 1990 (Nicholas Denton).

60 For the background, see *The Economist*, 20 April 1991, supra; *Financial Times*, 2 March 1991 (Ian Hargreaves); *Newsweek*, 10 June 1991.

Chapter 5: Domestic political effects

1 On the failure to monitor the budget deficit, see Anders Åslund, 'Is there any hope for Soviet reform?', *The World Today* (RIIA, London), July 1991, pp. 108ff.

2 Both these polls were quoted in *Moscow News*, No. 38, 1991.

3 *AiF*, No. 37, 1989.

4 See, for example, the comparative international tables of life expectation and infant mortality in *Naselenie SSSR. 1988* (Moscow: Finansy i statistika, 1989), pp. 694-6.

5 *Pravda*, 17 May 1988.

6 *Izvestiya*, 10 June 1988; *The Independent*, 11 June 1988 (Rupert Cornwell).

7 V.P. Ostrovsky et al., *Istoriya SSSR: Uchebnik dlya 11 klassa srednei shkoly* (Moscow: Prosveshchenie, 1990). The quotation from Andrei Sakharov is on pp. 199-200.

8 See Alexander Yakovlev in *Pravda*, 18 August 1989.

9 *Novyi mir*, No. 7, 1989, p. 183 (Andranik Migranyan).

10 Quoted by Professor Jim Riordan, *Life After Communism? The Cost to Russia and the World of the Failure of an Experiment*, inaugural lecture published by the University of Surrey, March 1991. The quotation is on p. 5.

11 See *Dialog*, No. 17, 1990, p. 3 (Andrei Zdravomyslov).

12 *International Herald Tribune*, 12 September 1989.

13 *Ibid.*, 17 January 1990.

14 *Ibid.*, 24-25 December 1990.

15 For example, *Moscow News*, No. 41, 1991, carried the front-page headline: 'Coup No. 2: last summer's farce may become the tragedy of next spring'.

16 One of the most extreme voices of this kind of anti-semitism is the weekly *Russkoye Voskresenie*, associated with the late K.V. Ostashvili-Smirnov. For a recent historical analysis of the nationalist phenomenon, see Stephen K. Carter, *Russian Nationalism: Yesterday, Today, Tomorrow* (London: Pinter Publishers, in association with John Spiers, 1990).

17 See *Literaturnaya gazeta*, 22 May 1991; *SWB (SU)* 13 June 1991. On a later occasion, however, Zhirinovsky described the Bolshevik Revolution as 'a tragic mistake': *Literaturnaya gazeta*, 6 November 1991.

18 BBC Monitoring Report, 18 June 1991.

19 *Moscow News*, No. 38, 1991 (Professor Yury Levada).

20 See Elizabeth Fuller, 'The Georgian Presidential Elections', RFE/RL

Report on the USSR, 7 June 1991, pp. 20f.

21 See Carla Thorson, 'RSFSR Forms Constitutional Court', RFE/RL *Report on the USSR*, 20 December 1991, pp. 13-16.

22 The text of Yeltsin's decree is published in *SWB (SU)*, 8 November 1991, quoting TASS World Service on 6 November. The grounds for the ban were that the Soviet Communist Party had 'never been a party' but was merely a mechanism for exercising power through the state structures; and that while the party's structures existed there could be no guarantee against another coup. However, since the party had already been suspended and its property sealed off since the August coup, it is not clear why its fate could not have been decided in accordance with the 1990 Soviet 'Law on Public Associations', Article 22 of which says that the dissolution of a party is a matter for the courts. For the text of this law, see *Novye zakony SSSR*, Vol. 3 (Moscow: Yuridicheskaya Literatura, 1991), pp. 18ff. Yeltsin's November decree was meant to be permanent – unlike the emergency measures taken against the party immediately after the August coup.

23 *Moscow News*, No. 1, 1992.

24 See Julia Wischnewsky, 'Russia: Liberal Media Criticize Democrats in Power', *RFE/RL Research Report*, 10 January 1992, p. 11, for examples.

25 See Julia Wischnewsky, 'Russians Gripped by "Court Fever"', *RFE/RL Research Report*, 6 March 1992, p. 1. The possibility of a trial was mentioned on 10 February 1992 by Evgeny Lisov, Russia's Deputy Prosecutor. Yakovlev has stated that he has been threatened with prosecution: see *Izvestiya*, 15 February 1992.

26 See *Dialog*, No. 5, 1991, p. 5; and No. 9, 1991, p. 58 (poll).

27 *Novyi mir*, No. 7, 1990, p. 185 (Lev Simkin). The author quoted a court case where, under public pressure, a defendant charged with murder and rape was tried and sentenced to death in a sports stadium in the presence of a large crowd. The case seems not to have been unique.

28 *Literaturnaya gazeta*, 9 January 1991.

29 *Ibid.*, 22 May 1991.

30 In late 1990, according to one estimate, 25 per cent of the Soviet population was living below the poverty line; see *AiF*, No. 45, 1990. The proportion is now very much higher.

31 *Literaturnaya gazeta*, 12 September 1990 (Vladimir Sokolov).

Chapter 6: Russian openness and the outside world

1 Hedrick Smith, *The New Russians* (London, Sydney, Auckland and Johannesburg: Hutchinson, 1990), p. 532.

2 *International Herald Tribune*, 29 July 1991.

3 *AiF*, No. 36, 1991.

4 *Pravda*, 7 November 1982 (Professor V.V. Zagladin).

5 *Izvestiya*, 18 January 1986 (Alexander Bovin); and *Pravda* 30 March 1987, quoted in Vera Tolz, 'Calls for Change in Soviet Reporting on Foreign Affairs', *Radio Liberty Research*, RL 328/87, 5 August 1987.

6 *Mirovaya ekonomika i mezhdunarodnye otnosheniya*, No. 11, 1987, p. 21.

7 *Vestnik ministerstva inostrannykh del*, 15 August 1988, p. 40. I am grateful to Margot Light for drawing my attention to the source here and in the previous footnote.

8 *Literaturnaya gazeta*, 15 June 1988 (V. Israelyan).

9 *Vestnik ministerstva inostrannykh del*, supra, p. 45.

10 See, for example, *Literaturnaya gazeta*, 2 May 1990 (Fyodor Burlatsky).

11 Based on an analysis of four issues of the weekly *Knizhnoye obozrenie*, for June and August 1991, respectively.

12 See the journals *Neva*, Nos. 7-8, 1988 (Koestler); *Novyi mir*, Nos. 2-4, 1989 (Orwell); *ibid.*, No. 10, 1989 (Conquest); and *ibid.*, No. 7, 1991 (Hayek). The remaining examples are taken from various issues of the weekly publication *Novye knigi SSSR* for 1989, 1990 and 1991.

13 *Independent on Sunday*, 25 August 1991, Supplement, p. 4 (Neal Ascherson).

14 See *SWB (SU)*, 24 August 1991 (Gorbachev mentions BBC and thanks journalists); and *ibid.*, 26 August 1991 (his reference to hearing a BBC correspondent reporting from the Russian parliament).

15 This finding was revealed by the head of the project, Dr Vladimir Shlapentokh, after his emigration to the United States in 1979; see Ellen Mickiewicz, *Media and the Russian Public* (New York: Praeger, 1981), p. 139.

16 See Eugene Parta, 'Soviet Area Audience and Opinion Research (SAAOR) at Radio Free Europe/Radio Liberty', in K.R.M. Short, ed., *Western Broadcasting over the Iron Curtain* (London and Sydney: Croom Helm, 1987), p. 231.

17 Ellen Mickiewicz, *Media and the Russian Public*, supra, p. 142, quoting a 1979 Radio Liberty Audience Research Analysis Report, 2-79, pp. 4-5.

18 These figures are quoted from *Radio Liberty Reports* AR 2-88, p. 16 and AR 1-90, p. 2, which cover the period to the end of 1989.

19 See 'The BBC in the USSR: Survey in Moscow, Leningrad and Kiev April 1990' (prepared by the International and Audience Research department of the BBC World Service, 1990; I am grateful for their permission to quote this).

20 Information provided by the Audience Research department of the BBC World Service.

21 See John Tusa, 'The BBC and Change in the Soviet Bloc', lecture at Regent's Park College, London, 21 March 1990 (BBC World Service Press Release, 1990). The quotations from Solzhenitsyn and Amalrik are on pp. 8-9.

22 The interviews with Professor Grushin and the other BBC listener were conducted in Moscow in March 1990. The conversation with Professor Levada was in Britain the following July.

23 Quoted by John Tusa, supra (n. 21), p. 16.

24 *The Times*, 6 June 1989 (Ian Murray from Bonn).

25 See Michael Clarke, *British External Policy-making in the 1990s* (London: Royal Institute of InternationalAffairs/Macmillan, forthcoming, 1992), pp. 335, 333.

26 *The Mail on Sunday*, 1 November 1987.

27 *International Herald Tribune* 15 December 1987 ('Gorbachev Tops Reagan in US Poll', quoting the *Washington Post*-ABC News Survey).

28 *Newsweek* Poll, *Newsweek*, 21 December 1987.

29 *The Guardian*, 2 March 1976 ('Solzhenitsyn's awful warning'). A fuller, although apparently incomplete, text of the interview appeared in *The Listener*, 4 March 1976, pp. 260f.

30 Oskar Morgenstern, *The Question of National Defense* (New York: Random House, 1959), pp. 289-90.

31 Michael Herman, 'The Role of Military Intelligence since 1945'. Paper delivered to the Seminar on Twentieth Century British Politics and Administration, Institute of Historical Research, University of London, 24 May 1989, p. 9. Mr Herman is a former member of the Defence Intelligence Staff.

Chapter 7: A more open world

1 *Pravda*, 24 May 1991; *The Times*, 5 July 1991 (leading article) and 9 November 1991 (Mary Dejevsky).

2 According to one sceptical media specialist: 'For most, politics is of marginal concern, and surveys show that people very quickly become bored with too much information'; see Terence H. Qualter, *Opinion Control in the Democracies* (London: Macmillan in association with the London School of Economics, 1985), p. 243. This book contains an extensive review of the relevant findings on the media's impact.

3 *New York Times Magazine*, 10 November 1985, p. 48 (David Shipler).

4 Alastair Buchan, *Conflict and Communication*, seventh Noel Buxton
Lecture at the University of Essex, 2 March 1971 (London: Longman for
the University of Essex). The passages quoted are on pp. 11-12, 14 and 16-17.

5 Asa Briggs, *The History of Broadcasting in the United Kingdom*, Vol. III,
The War of Words (London, New York and Toronto: Oxford University
Press, 1970), p. 77 (footnote).

6 *The Times*, 5 December 1990.

7 *Literaturnaya gazeta*, 9 January 1991 (Fyodor Burlatsky).

8 *Pechat' v SSSR v 1986 godu* (Moscow: Finansy i statistika, 1987), pp. 116,
106.

9 See Mikhail Poltoranin, in the Moscow newspaper *Trud*, 14 January 1992.

10 RFE/RL *Report on the USSR*, 4 January 1991, Introduction.

11 See House of Commons, *Second Report from the Foreign Affairs Committee. Session 1985-86. UK-Soviet Relations*, Vol. 1 (London: HMSO, 1986),
p. lix-lxiii, paras 540-54, for a review of this trend.

12 See Norman Wooding, Bryan Cartledge and Malcolm Jones, 'Review of
Soviet and East European Studies', July 1989.

13 *The Times*, 29 June 1990 (letter from authors mentioned in note 12).

14 House of Commons, *UK-Soviet Relations*, supra (n. 11), p. lxii.

15 *The Times*, 10 May 1990 (report by Andrew McEwen).

16 See Ronald Amman, 'The future of Soviet studies: the political perspective', *Journal of Communist Studies*, Vol. 7, No. 3, September 1991,
p. 378.

17 See Bernard Pares, in A.W. Ward et al., eds, *The Cambridge Modern
History*, Vol. XII (Cambridge: at the University Press, 1910), pp. 330f. The
author correctly says of Bolshevik policy that 'terrorism was condemned as
impotent and disintegrating ... though Lenin and his friends did not shrink
from the idea of an ultimate insurrection'; *ibid.*, p. 331.

18 *International Herald Tribune*, 4 October 1990.

19 Stalin's remark was made in May 1935 to the then French Foreign
Minister, Pierre Laval, who had suggested that Stalin should do something to encourage the Catholics. See Winston Churchill, *The Second
World War*, Vol. I, *The Gathering Storm* (London: Cassell and Co.,
1948), p. 105. I am grateful to Stephen White for his help in locating this
quotation.

20 Thomas C. Schelling, *The Strategy of Conflict* (London, Oxford and New
York: Oxford University Press, 1960), p. 4.

21 James Baker, 'The Euro-Atlantic Architecture: From East to West'.
Address delivered to the Aspen Institute in Berlin, 18 June 1991 (official
text issued by the USIS Reference Center, London, pp. 1, 7, 8).

Notes

22 *International Herald Tribune*, 26 June 1991 (William Pfaff, 'Baker's Commonwealth of Democracies').

Chapter 8: Conclusion

1 The sizes of the former British and French colonial empires are calculated from *Whitaker's Almanack*, 1939, pp. 642, 957.
2 See *The Independent*, 29 April 1989 for the full text of this speech, which was delivered to the Bundestag two days earlier.
3 See Vaclav Havel in *International Herald Tribune*, 15 July 1991 (quoting his speech of 1990).
4 See William Schneider, 'Public Opinion', in Joseph S. Nye, Jr., ed., *The Making of America's Soviet Policy* (New Haven and London: Yale University Press, 1984), pp. 18-19.
5 See David Wedgwood Benn, *Persuasion and Soviet Politics* (Oxford: Basil Blackwell, 1989), p. 140.